$1.95

The Primitive World
and Its Transformations

BY ROBERT REDFIELD

The Primitive World and Its Transformations

The Primitive World and Its Transformations

By ROBERT REDFIELD

Cornell Paperbacks

CORNELL UNIVERSITY PRESS

ITHACA, NEW YORK

Acknowledgments

I THANK the Committee on University Lectures at Cornell University for the opportunity to give the lectures which became this book and for permission to repeat certain parts of them at the University of Paris; Claude Tardits and Eric de Dampierre for suggestions as to the thought given in the course of translating those parts into French; Robert J. Braidwood and Linda S. Braidwood for reading the manuscript and offering excellent advice; my daughter, Lisa Peattie, for ideas and facts provided in the course of developing Chapters IV and VI; Charles Leslie for much careful help in finding sources in the library and making good use of them; and Zelda Leslie for patient and intelligent work in preparing the manuscript for the publisher.

Part of the substance of Chapter IV has been published in "The Primitive World View," *Proceedings of the American Philosophical Society*, XCVI (February, 1952).

◇◇◇

Contents

"The new mentality is more important even than
the new science and the new technology."

—A. N. WHITEHEAD

Introduction

IN THESE pages I consider certain of the changes that
were brought about in mankind by the advent of civilization. After the rise of cities men became something different
from what they had been before. History is here conceived
as the story of a single career, that of the human race. The
emphasized event in that career, the turning point in the
changes which mankind has undergone, is the passage
from precivilized to civilized life. In the wide view here
to be taken, the several thousands of years during which
the first cities rose in half a dozen places become a single
happening, the coming of civilization. I seek to understand
something of what this change meant generally, for all of
us, for humanity as if humanity were one man slowly
changing throughout many millenniums before civilization
and then coming of age in a transition profoundly effective
and relatively abrupt.

In this search I have been guided by a choice of themes
and the influence of certain writers. In several notable
books, Professor V. Gordon Childe [1] has reviewed the coming of civilization, especially in the Old World, and has told
us that there have been times when changes, especially in
technology, have been relatively rapid and far-reaching in
their results. Such changes he calls "revolutions." I have

adopted his use of that word, but with hesitation; I have substituted, in several contexts, the word "transformation." For the abruptness of the changes in which Childe is interested is in some doubt, and the abruptness of the changes in which I am interested I do not even assert. Childe's three great revolutions—the food-producing, the urban, and the industrial—are revolutions primarily or largely in technology. That cities rose rapidly in proportion to the time it took for man to reach the period of city building is clear. But not all archaeologists would recognize two marked accelerations in the upward curve of technological development in the Old World. Reviewing the archaeological record in Iraq, Robert Braidwood [2] sees but one important acceleration in the development of technology. He tells us that after the coming of agriculture and animal husbandry, the manner of life changed from that of roving collectors of wild foods to that of settled farmers, and that these farmers began to add the technological characteristics of civilization—town life, markets, organized religion, and so forth—a little at a time, so that the ancient Middle Eastern village dweller became a town dweller and then a city man in a course of development that showed its energy before cities were built and continued in a smooth acceleration into full civilization.

For the interests expressed in these pages, it is not necessary to decide between a single or a double technological revolution in prehistoric times. I have turned to the possibility that we might recognize in the changing human career important and far-reaching changes in the habits of men's minds. Here I have been one of the many influenced by the writings of A. N. Whitehead; his treatment of some great historic changes in the ways men have come to use their minds has contributed to the organization of my thought its idealistic, rather than materialist, emphasis.

√ The third theme or point of view that will soon become apparent is derived from my experience as a student of the primitive and peasant peoples. These pages recount some episodes in the story of civilization as it is told from the bottom up, so to speak. I shall begin with the primitive peoples and write about them as they became or are becoming something else. The people with written histories are what the preliterate peoples have become. I look forward from precivilized life to civilization.

The peoples who existed before the rise of the first cities can be conveniently referred to as the precivilized peoples. For the peoples that the ethnologist studies today, there is no term free from criticism. Even the neutral "preliterate" will not quite do, for there are some peoples who have had for a long time some use of reading and writing and yet show none of the consequences of literacy which we find in civilized societies. I shall use "primitive" and "preliterate" interchangeably. I shall also use the phrase "folk society." I shall say that the societies that existed before the rise of cities "were folk societies," and I shall say that the societies that are found today unaffected by the great civilizations "are folk societies." [3] By this I shall simply mean that, as compared with civilized societies, the precivilized societies did, and the present-day primitive societies do, exhibit certain characteristics—and the same characteristics—that distinguish them from civilized societies. The characteristics will soon be named: isolation, homogeneity, and so forth. The distinctions are in degree, but they are important. The constructed type of a fictitious or ideal folk society which has been set forth in other writings [4] is in these pages no more than a provider of suggestions for characterizing real societies seen by the ethnologist or encountered more remotely by the archaeologist.

In the first chapter I shall try to describe the conditions of human living that must have prevailed before civilization began. The second chapter will be a sketchy account of what happened to the precivilized and primitive societies after civilization had come into existence. The third chapter rests upon a distinction which I shall make in general terms in the first chapter, the distinction between the technical order and the moral order. In the third chapter something will be said about the disintegration of the local moral orders that takes place in civilization; I shall also refer to the rise, with civilization, of more inclusive moral orders. This seems to me a very important change in human affairs. With this great change I associate what could be distinguished as a second transformation—the rise of ideas as forces in history, influencing the moral order directly. This theme belongs to the historians of ideas; I do not venture to discuss it. In the fourth chapter I shall be concerned with the transformation of a primitive world view wherein man comes at last to confront a universe empty of personality and indifferent to men. Here too I shall contribute little from my own stock of knowledge, but state, perhaps in an enlarged context, something which scholars have studied in detail. The fifth chapter will take up the appearance and development of man's assumed competence to construct himself and society by deliberate design. We might here speak of the transformation in self-management. The last chapter deals with one aspect of this change whereby man comes to assume responsibility for fashioning his world; it will be concerned with the effect of civilization in altering the standards by which man judges that human conduct is good or bad. The last chapter strays a little from the course laid down by the others, for while the first five take for their facts what anthropologists (and others) have told me of what other people did or do, the materials which allow me in the last chapter to discuss the transformation of ethical judgment are the things that anthropologists do, as anthropologists.

I

Human Society
before the Urban Revolution

WHAT can be said that is general and true about the condition of mankind before civilization? The question is directed to a time from five to six thousand years ago. At that time human populations were to be found on all the world's continents, with the possible exception of Australia. Greenland had not yet been invaded by man, and some of the islands of the Pacific were as yet without human occupants. But there were people in a great many widely scattered parts of the habitable earth, not very many of them in any one place, and not very many of them altogether. No city had yet been built anywhere.

The question is whether anything can be said, with show of reason and evidence, about *all* the human beings that were there then, whether they lived in the arctic or in the tropics, whether they hunted, fished, or farmed, and whatever may have been the color of their skins, the languages they spoke, or the particular beliefs and customs that they had. The question demands a positive characterization of their manner of life. The description should be more than a mere statement of the things that those early men did not have that we today do have. It should say: this is what

1

they did; this is how they felt; this is the way the world looked to them.

The question, so understood, appears to require more than can be provided from trustworthy evidence, but I do not think that it really does. It can be answered from two sources of information. The archaeologists dig up the material things that men of those times made and used, and from these things draw reasonable inferences about their manner of life. And, secondly, the ethnologists tell us a good deal about the ways of life of those people who until recent times have remained uncivilized: the primitive, the preliterate—or, to use the old-fashioned terms— the savage and the barbaric peoples. To learn what pre-civilized men were like, we may look to the accounts of the remains of ancient camps and settlements unaffected by cities, either because they were there before there were any cities anywhere, or because they stood remote and unreached by ancient cities already arisen. And also we may look to what has been written in great detail about many hundreds of present-day tribes and bands and villages, little communities of the never civilized. I do not assume that these latter people have experienced no changes in the several thousands of years since the first cities were built. The particular thoughts and beliefs of the present-day preliterates have probably changed a good deal during many hundreds of generations. The customs of these people are not "earlier" [1] than is our own civilization, for they have had as long a history as have we. But what I do assert is that the surviving primitive peoples have remained substantially unaffected by civilization. Insofar as the conditions of primitive life remain—in the smallness of the community, and in its isolation and non-literacy—so, too, the kind of thoughts and beliefs, however

2

changed in specific content, remain of a kind characteristic of primitive society. That there is such a kind is evidenced to us from the fact that we can generalize as to this manner of thought and belief from the surviving primitive peoples, in the face of the very great variety of content of thought and belief which these exhibit. These surviving primitive peoples provide us with instances of that general and primordial kind of human living which it is my immediate purpose to describe.

Now it is fortunate for the present enterprise that these two sources of information, the archaeological and the ethnological, supplement each other. Where the former is weak, the latter is strong; and where the ethnologist may be insufficiently impressed by the influence of technology on the manner of life of a human community, the archaeologist can hardly fail to be impressed. This is what he sees: the material things. Moreover, of the many meanings which are locked in the artifacts that ancient peoples made, it is those meanings which relate to practical action, especially the getting of food, which communicate themselves most readily to the archaeologist who finds them. A Plains Indian medicine bundle or an Australian totemic design as an archaeological object by itself would convey only a little of the very great deal which the ethnologist who can talk to a living Indian or Australian can find out that it means. So the archaeologist's view of the manner of life of the precivilized peoples will emphasize the practical aspects of living and the material influences on change. An archaeologist should make a little effort to lean deliberately away from a materialist view of human life and a conception of history in simple terms of economic determinism. His work inclines him toward it. On the other hand, the ethnologist is often in a position where he can

3

find out little or nothing of the history of the people he is studying, as they have written nothing down about it, having no means to do so; and so it may sometimes appear to him that they are to be explained chiefly in terms of the kinds of marriage choices he finds them making when he finds them, or the potlatches they give. In the absence of a history, the way the material conditions of living limited that people here or gave them a chance to develop something there may not be apparent.

Archaeologist and ethnologist, however, do often talk to each other, and indeed in some cases are the same person. So the separation of work, the difference in emphasis, is not so great as I have perhaps made it sound. In the attempt to characterize the precivilized manner of life, I will begin by following Childe, an archaeologist. Professor Childe is interested in the effects on human development of changes in the technology by which food is produced. He makes a separation of importance between that period in human history when men were hunters and fishers only (savagery), and that period when men had learned how to be agriculturalists or animal breeders (barbarism). The change from the one kind of life to the other he calls a revolution, "the food-producing revolution."

The discovery of how to produce food was, of course, of enormous importance in human history, and it is not too much to call it a revolution and to group it, as Childe does, with the "urban revolution," when civilization came into being, and with the industrial revolution of modern times. Yet certain qualifications or additions need to be made. It has been pointed out that the food-producing revolution was the more notable event in that from the condition of food collecting one could not predict that food producing would be achieved, but that when once food production

4

had increased human population and made leisure possible, civilization was bound to come about.[2] And it is also necessary to recognize that some of the changes characteristic of each stage may have taken place, in one community or another, before the revolution in technology that Childe stresses had occurred there. Thus we know that a sedentary village life is possible to a people who know nothing of agriculture or animal husbandry. The fishing Indians of our Northwest coast lived a village life and developed certain aspects of their culture very highly. In prehistoric times there existed on the Scandinavian coast sessile communities, quite comparable with Neolithic farmers in the village character of life, with pottery and the polishing of flint, but without crops or herds.[3] Also, it is not unlikely that with the advent of agriculture there began some of those changes which we are able to see only when cities and writing have made them visible to us. The excavations in Iraq, already mentioned, suggest this possibility. As the changes in technology, so also the changes in the human mind which are the subject of these pages may have well begun before the urban revolution, even before the food-producing revolution.

Nevertheless, within the wide generalizations that I am here attempting, the food-producing revolution and the urban revolution may be considered as two parts of one great transformation. To one interested in changes in human habits and capacities of mind, the urban revolution is the more important part, for it is with the coming of city life that we are able to see novel and transforming attitudes taken toward life and the universe. That these novel attitudes began earlier is likely, and farther on in these pages indications will be drawn from present-day primitive societies that occasional beginnings of these civilized attitudes were to be found in the precivilized societies had we been there to look for them. The question as to the relative importance of Childe's two first revolutions may be set aside with this statement: the food-producing revolution was perhaps the turning point in the human career, but it was through the urban revolution that the consequences of the turn were realized.

Now let us attempt a characterization of mankind in precivilized times. Let us begin with the simple statement that in the primary condition of mankind the human community was small. As Childe says, writing of the food-collecting period, hunters and vegetable-food collectors usually live in small roving bands.[4] Even the more stable settlement of Pacific coast Indian fishing people, of recent times exceptionally well provided with food, includes hardly more than thirty occupied houses and several hundred people. Nor does the immediate transition to food producing increase substantially the size of the community, now a group of farmer's huts or a center of cattle raising.

On the whole the growth of population was not reflected so much in the enlargement of the settlement unit as in a multiplication of settlements. In ethnography neolithic villages can boast only a few hundred inhabitants. . . . In prehistoric Europe the largest neolithic village yet known, Barkaer in Jutland, comprised fifty-two small, one-roomed dwellings, but sixteen to thirty houses was a more normal figure; so the average local group in neolithic times would average two hundred to four hundred members.[5]

Certain food-producing town centers well on the way to civilization do give indication of larger populations, but hunters' bands or food producers' settlements are alike in general contrast to the far larger community which was the ancient city with its seven thousand to twenty thousand inhabitants.[6] What is here worth emphasizing is that until the rise of civilization mankind lived in communities so small that every adult could, and no doubt did, know everybody else.

These communities were isolated from one another. Again Childe gives us to understand that the change in this regard with the coming of agriculture was a change in some degree, but at first not a radical change. Throughout both Paleolithic and Neolithic times each little group was largely self-contained and self-supported, as the surviving primitive societies, whether hunters or growers of vegetable or animal food, are largely self-contained and self-supported. The trade that occurred in Paleolithic times was chiefly trade in nonessentials; with Neolithic times the trade intensified and included some staple commodities, such as stone for querns and flint for hand axes.[7] But the trade did not greatly limit the essential separateness of the local community. The isolation of the Neolithic settlement continued into the medieval English village.[8] Villagers of primitives or peasants today are still relatively isolated, and, on the whole, when such people have more than casual association with outsiders, it is with people who are much like themselves, in neighboring bands or settlements that are like their own community.

So we may characterize mankind in its primary condition as living in small and isolated communities. These communities were of course without writing. I do not say more of this absence of literacy and literature; its importance as a criterion of primitive as contrasted with civilized living is familiar. To these qualities others may be added. The precivilized community was composed of one kind of people. If this fact is not to be deduced from the archaeol-

7

ogist's data, it follows from what we know of isolated primitive communities seen today. Small and isolated communities are intimate communities; people come to have the same ways of doing things; they marry with and live almost entirely with others like them in that community.

Next we may say that the members of the precivilized community had a strong sense of group solidarity. No doubt they thought of themselves as naturally belonging together, and so far as they were aware of people different from themselves, they thought their own ways to be better than those of the ways of others. These things also may be said, not only because they are necessary consequences of the isolation and the smallness of the community, but because we see them to be true of contemporary primitive communities. Civilized communities are more heterogeneous, and the sense of group solidarity is qualified by the number and variety of kinds of groups to which the individual makes attachment—or by the difficulty of making firm attachments to groups in some urban situations.

Let us follow Professor Childe further in his characterization of precivilized man. We see that now he must make increasing use of reasonable deduction and of the evidence from ethnology. He tells us that in the precivilized community there were no full-time specialists. He asserts this for the reason that in communities with simple hunting or even farming "there simply will not be enough food to go round unless every member of the group contributes to the supply." [9] In the primitive societies of the present day there are rarely full-time specialists. So the assumption is fairly well founded that in the early condition of mankind what men did was customarily different from what women did, but what one man did was much like what another did. There were men with special skills at activities carried

8

on by all men, and there were probably shamans or other part-time practitioners in the spiritual and healing arts. Differences among individuals with respect to the depth of understanding of cosmogonic and religious ideas may have been very considerable; this is a matter to which we shall recur on a later page. But, on the whole, all men shared the same essential knowledge, practiced the same arts of life, had the same interests and similar experiences.

Yet another characteristic of precivilized living may be asserted. Within those early communities the relationships among people were primarily those of personal status. In a small and intimate community all people are known for their individual qualities of personality. Few or no strangers take part in the daily life. So men and women are seen as persons, not as parts of mechanical operations, as city people see so many of those around them. Indeed, this disposition to see what is around one as human and personal like oneself is not, in precivilized or primitive society, limited to people; a great deal of what we call "nature" is more or less so regarded. The cosmos is personal and human-like.

Also in this connection it may be said that the groupings of people within the primitive community is one that depends on status and on role, not on mere practical usefulness. There are fathers, or older people, or shamans, or priests; each such kind of person is accorded prestige. In civilized societies the network of relationships of utility— the numbers and kinds of people who produce goods and services are so great and are at such remote distances—that many of the relationships that keep people provided with what they use are not involved in status at all, for those who use the goods. In primitive societies the status relationships are universal and dominant; the exceptions to be made would be those relatively few that arise out of trade with foreign communities.

Furthermore, in this personal universe where categories of relationships involve status, the forms and groupings of kinship provide the basic classifications. The original human society was one of kinsmen. Childe speaks of the "sentiment of kinship" [10] which in considerable part held the group together. Within the precivilized society, it is safe to assume that relationships were essentially familial. The primary arrangements of personal status and role are those connected with that universally persistent kind of family anthropologists now call "nuclear" and the extensions of this primary kinship into many, possibly even all, of the other relationships within the community. Moreover, the categories of kinship may include elements of nature, as some animals, and supernatural beings. Of course we cannot say just what were the kinship institutions in the thousands of bands and settlements that constituted precivilized society. In his latest book Childe [11] with ingenuity and prudence draws reasonable inferences as to elements of social organization in precivilized societies known only archaeologically. The result suggests the presence in one place of single-family households, in another of large households including several or many nuclear families, and a variety of forms of marriage. Nevertheless the very smallness and isolation of the precivilized community everywhere allows us to say that in the early condition of humanity, the community, as well as the cosmos of which its members felt it to be a part, was essentially made up of personal relationships, and that the patterning of these relationships was primarily accomplished by developments derived from the differences of age, sex, and familial connection. Today, among western Australian peoples, "the whole society forms a body of relatives," [12] and the intimate connection between the body of relatives and nature, through the water hole or other center of animal multiplication, and the totemic rites, is familiar to readers of Australian ethnology.

What, essentially, held together this primordial human community? Was it the mutual usefulness to one another of those few hunters or fishers or farmers? To answer, Yes, is to recognize what is obviously true: "Cooperation is essential to secure food and shelter and for defense against foes, human and subhuman." [13] But to answer, Yes, is also to suggest a possible misconception. The "identity of economic interests" of which Childe writes in the paragraph in which he so interestingly characterizes the mode of life of man before civilization, is a fact which any of us would have observed had we been there to see the precivilized community, and which is an obvious inference from what we know more directly about it. But this does not mean that in those communities men worked primarily for material wealth. The incentives to work and to exchange labor and goods are, in primitive and precivilized society especially, various and chiefly noneconomic (in the narrow sense). They arise from tradition, from a sense of obligation coming out of one's position in a system of status relationships, especially those of kinship, and from religious considerations and moral motivations of many kinds. The point has been put very convincingly by Karl Polanyi.[14] Let us then add to our characterization of the precivilized society that it was a society in which the economy was one determined by status (as contrasted with the society imagined and in part realized in nineteenth-century Europe and America, in which the economy was determined by the market). In the precivilized or the primitive society "man's economy is, as a rule, submerged in his social relations." [15] Essentially and primarily, man "does not aim at safeguarding his individual interest in the acquisition of material possessions, but rather at ensuring social good-will, social status, social assets. He values possessions primarily as a means to that end." We are talking now of a time before the acquisitive society.

To answer only that the precivilized community was held together by reason of mutual usefulness is to fail to say what it is that most importantly and characteristically holds such a community together. Indeed, Childe sees and states succinctly, in terms which Durkheim caused many of us to use, the difference in this regard between the precivilized settlement and the city. It is not the former, but the earliest cities that "illustrate a first approximation to an organic solidarity based upon functional complementarity and interdependence between all its members such as subsist between the constituent cells of an organism." [16] It is the urban community that rests upon mutual usefulness. The primitive and precivilized communities are held together essentially by common understandings as to the ultimate nature and purpose of life. The precivilized society was like the present-day primitive society in those characteristics—isolation, smallness, homogeneity, persistence in the common effort to make a way of living under relatively stable circumstances—to which we have already attended, and therefore it was like the parallel societies which we can observe today in that its fundamental order was a matter of moral conviction. In both cases the society

exists not so much in the exchange of useful functions as in common understandings as to the ends given. The ends are not stated as matters of doctrine, but are implied by the many acts which make up the living that goes on in the society. Therefore, the morale of a folk society—its power to act consistently over periods of time and to meet crises effectively—is not dependent upon discipline exerted by force or upon devotion to some single principle of action, but to the concurrence and consistency of many or all of the actions and conceptions which make up the whole round of life.[17]

For the homogeneity of such a society is not that homogeneity in which everybody does the same thing at the same time.[18] The people are homogeneous in that they share the same tradition and have the same view of the good life. They do the same kinds of work and they worship and marry and feel shame or pride in the same way and under similar circumstances. But at any one time the members of a primitive community may be doing notably different things: the women looking for edible roots while the men hunt; some men out on a war party while others at home perform a rite for its success. And when there is a familial ceremonial, or a magico-religious ritual affecting the whole community, the differences in what is being done may be very great. In the activities to gain a material living, labor, as between man and man or woman and woman, may be divided. But the total specialization of function, as among people of different sexes and age-or-kinship positions, and as among participants in a rite, may be very considerable. The point to be stressed is that all these activities conduce to a purpose, express a view of man's duty, that all share, and to which each activity or element of institution contributes.

We can safely say these things of the precivilized societies as we can say them of the primitive societies because these things follow from the other characteristics which we have already conceded, and are attested in every very isolated, undisturbed primitive society we observe today.

13

For the same reasons it is possible to add yet other attributes to the characterization. In the most primitive societies of living men into which we may enter and which we can come directly to understand, the controls of action are informal; they rest on the traditional obligations of largely inherited status, and are expressed in talk and gesture and in the patterns of reciprocal action. Political institutions are few and simple, or even entirely absent. The members of these societies "believe in the sacred things; their sense of right and wrong springs from the unconscious roots of social feeling, and is therefore unreasoned, compulsive and strong." [19] People do the kind of things they do, not because somebody just thought up that kind of thing, or because anybody ordered them to do so, but because it seems to the people to flow from the very necessity of existence that they do that kind of thing. The reasons given after the thing is done, in the form of myth and the dress of ceremony, assert the rightness of the choice. Particular things are done as a result of decision as to that particular action, but as to the class of action, tradition is the source and the authority. "The Indians decide now to go on a hunt; but it is not a matter of debate whether one should, from time to time, hunt." [20] So the principles of rightness which underlie the activities are largely tacit. And they are not the subject of much explicit criticism, nor even of very much reflective thought. Institutions are not planned out, nor is their modification a matter of much deliberate choice and action. Legislation, though it may occur, is not the characteristic form of legal action in primitive societies. And what Malinowski [21] refers to as "science" in connection with the primitive peoples is better distinguished as practical knowledge. And these things too may with confidence be attributed to the precivilized societies.

Yet, because in them thought and action were largely traditional and uncritical, it does not follow that activities were automatic or empty of meaning. Rather we must suppose that activity with them as with us involved lively and variable subjective states. Ruth Bunzel, studying Pueblo potters, found that the Indian woman who was in fact copying the designs of other potters with only the smallest variation was unaware that she copied, condemned copying as wrong, and had a strong conviction that she was in fact inventive and creative.[22] And as for the meaning of life—that was, so to speak, guaranteed. One did what tradition said one did, making a multitude of interesting and particular choices. But all of it fell within and was motivated by the common understandings of the little community as to the nature and purpose of life.

The attempt to gather together some of the attributes of that form of human living which prevailed before the first civilizations arose may now be halted. Later we shall examine some of the respects in which it is necessary to qualify this characterization. Enough of the characterization for the needs of these pages has been assembled. There results a picture, very generalized, of the organization of life, social control, and motivation among most of the societies of mankind during most of human history. The point upon which we are to insist, for its importance in considering the topics of the following lectures, is that in this early condition of humanity the essential order of society, the nexus which held people together, was moral. Humanity attained its characteristic, long-enduring nature as a multitude of different but equivalent systems of relationships and institutions each expressive of a view of the good. Each pre-civilized society was held together by largely undeclared but continually realized ethical conceptions.

15

Professor Childe unfortunately happened upon a figure of comparison that leads in the direction just opposite to the truth when he wrote that the solidarity of the precivilized community was "really based on the same principles as that of a pack of wolves or a herd of sheep." [23] Even the little glimpses of religion and sense of obligation to do right which are accorded the archaeologist show us that twenty-five thousand years ago the order of society was moral order. That of wolves or sheep is not. Childe's facts prove that this was so and that his comparison of precivilized society with that of animals is misleading. Describing the wall paintings, the personal adornments, the trade in cowrie shells, and the hints these things give of a life of the mind and the spirit among the Western Europeans of the Ice Age, Childe says, "Savagery produced a dazzling culture." [24] It is Childe who uses this adjective for the cultures at the end of the Ice Age that found expression in necklaces of animal teeth, in well-executed realistic paintings of the animals that were hunted, in stone-weighted skeletons of reindeer cast into a German lake, "presumably as an offering to the spirit of the herd or the genius of the land," according to Childe.

The antiquity of the moral order is not fully attested by archaeology. A people's conceptions as to the good are only meagerly represented in the material things that they make. A tribe of western Australia, the Pitjendadjara, today carry on a religious and moral life of great intensity, but they make and use material objects so few and so perishable that were these people exhibited to us only through archaeology, we would barely know that they had existed and we would know nothing of their moral life. As described by Charles P. Mountford in his charming book,[25] these aborigines perform their rites to increase animal and plant food, and they follow a morality of personal relations with dignity and conscience. Mountford says that they make but five tools: a spear, a spear thrower, a wooden carrying dish, a stone slab on which to grind food, and a digging stick. Perhaps this investigator overlooked some of the articles made by these aborigines, but it is certainly true that naked and wandering, with almost none of the material possessions and power which we associate with the development of humanity, they are nevertheless as human as are you and I.

We may suppose that fifty thousand years ago mankind had developed a variety of moral orders, each expressed in some local tradition, and comparable to what we find among aborigines today. Their development required both the organic evolution of human bodily and cerebral nature and also the accumulation of experience by tradition. As the tradition began to accumulate while the organic evolution was still going on, the moral order—and the technical order—began to be established among the apelike men of the early Pleistocene. On the other hand, until bodily and cerebral nature equivalent to that of men living today had been developed, we cannot fairly attribute to those earliest humanoid societies a moral order comparable, let us say, with that of the Australian blackfellow. Even in the case of so relatively late a being as Neanderthal man there was a factor of biological difference which would have limited the development of culture. But by a time seventy-five or fifty thousand years ago, the biological evolution of mankind had reached a point at which the genetic qualities necessary for the development of fully human life had been attained. This reaches the conclusion that for a period of time at least five times as long as the entire period of civilization man has had the capacity for a life governed by such moral orders as we see in primitive societies today. The men who left the paintings of Altamira were fully human and not very different from us. And I follow Eliseo Vivas when he writes:

That does not mean, of course, that they pursued the identical values and were capable of the same theoretical sophistication of which we are capable; it merely means that they probably had the same degree of moral sensibility, though perhaps focused toward different objects than those toward which we, the men of contemporary technological society, focus ours.[26]

In recognizing that every precivilized society of the past fifty or seventy-five millenniums had a moral order to which the technical order was subordinate, I do not say that the religious and ethical systems of these societies were equally complex. Then, as now, there were "thin cultures" and "rich cultures." Childe sees certain of the mesolithic cultures as "thin" in comparison with the cultures that preceded them. It is not, of course, clear that the thinness lay in the moral life. Maybe they had a religious and personal life that is not represented in the archaeology. However this may be in that particular case, we are to recognize that the development of technology had, even in precivilized times, an important influence on the moral life. While the Australians show us how little material culture is needed for the development of a moral order, such a contrast as that between the Haida and the Paiute Indians reminds us that generally speaking a people desperately concerned with getting a living cannot develop a rich moral or esthetic life. The moral order of a hard-pressed people may be itself simple. But I insist that it is there in every case.

One other point is to be made about the moral orders that preceded civilization. Morality has had its developmental history. I shall return to this development in the last chapter. Here I say that when the moralities of primitive or precivilized peoples are judged by men of the present day, some are found to be better than others; and the judgment makes allowances for practical difficulties encountered by the primitive people. In primitive societies known today where the food quest is all absorbing one does not condemn the people for failing to develop much creative art or for failing to show a particularly humane consideration for other people. The Siriono of Bolivia, as recently reported by Allen R. Holmberg,[27] live a harsh and precarious life in a tropical rain forest. They have their moral order—systems of intense inhibition as to sexual relations with certain relatives, ideas as to the rights and duties of relatives to share food, fearful attitudes toward invisible spirits, and so forth. But men's activities "remain on the same monotonous level day after day and year after year, and they are centered largely around the satisfaction of the basic needs of hunger, sex and avoidance of fatigue and pain." Holmberg saw a band of Indians walk out of a camp leaving a woman, sick to death, alone in her hammock. "Even the husband departed without saying goodbye." It is stern necessity that makes for this conduct; children, who can be cared for, are tenderly treated at much expenditure of effort. On the other hand, elsewhere we are reminded of the degree to which respect for personal integrity may develop among primitive food collectors. Among the Yagua, another people living under difficult conditions in the tropical forest of South America, although the entire clan lives in a single long house, Fejos tells us that the members of the large household "are able to obtain perfect privacy whenever they wish it simply by turning their faces to the wall of the house. Whenever a man, woman or child faces the wall, the others regard that individual as if he were no longer present." [28]

I turn now to the distinction between the technical order and the moral order, and from that proceed to contrast precivilized and primitive living with civilized living in terms of this distinction. Technical order and moral order name two contrasting aspects of all human societies. The phrases stand for two distinguishable ways in which the activities of men are co-ordinated. As used by C. H. Cooley [29] and R. E. Park,[30] "the moral order" refers to the organization of human sentiments into judgments as to what is right. Describing how the division of labor puts an organization of society based on occupation and vocational interests in place of an older kind of organization of society, Park contrasts these newer ties, based on common interests, with "forms of association like the neighborhood, which are based on contiguity, personal association, and the common ties of humanity." [31] The division of labor modifies this older moral order. Here we will extend the significance of the phrase, and make it cover all the binding together of men through implicit convictions as to what is right, through explicit ideals, or through similarities of conscience. The moral order is therefore always based on what is peculiarly human—sentiments, morality, conscience—and in the first place arises in the groups where people are intimately associated with one another. The word "values," [32] is a related conception, but the phrase "moral order" points to the nature of the bonds among men, rather than to a category of the content of culture. We may conceive of the moral order as equally present in those societies in which the rules for right conduct among men are supported by supernatural sanctions and in those in which the morality of human conduct is largely independent of the religion (in the sense of belief and cult about the supernatural). "Moral order" includes the binding sentiments of rightness that attend religion, the social solidarity that accompanies religious ritual, the sense of religious seriousness and obligation that strengthens men, and the effects of a belief in invisible beings that embody goodness. The moral order becomes vivid to us when we think of the Australian Arunta assembling, each man to do his part, denying himself food, making the sacred marks or performing the holy dances, that the witchetty-grub may become numerous and the whole band thus continue to find its food. Or of the old Chinese family performing the rituals for the ancestors. Or of the members of the boys' gang refusing, even in the face of threats from the police, to "tell on" a fellow member.

By a corresponding extension of another and more familiar term, all the other forms of co-ordination of activity which appear in human societies may be brought together and contrasted with the moral order under the phrase "the technical order." The bonds that co-ordinate the activities of men in the technical order do not rest on convictions as to the good life; they are not characterized by a foundation in human sentiments; they can exist even without the knowledge of those bound together that they are bound together. The technical order is that order which results from mutual usefulness, from deliberate coercion, or from the mere utilization of the same means. In the technical order men are bound by things, or are themselves things. They are organized by necessity or expediency. Think, if you will, of the orderly way in which automobiles move in response to the traffic light or the policeman's whistle, or think of the flow of goods, services, and money among the people who together produce, distribute, and consume some commodity such as rubber.

Civilization may be thought of as the antithesis of the folk society. It may also, and consistently with the first antithesis, be thought of as that society in which the relations between technical order and moral order take forms radically different from the relationships between the two which prevail in precivilized society.

Civilization (conceived now as one single thing and not —as by Toynbee—as twenty-one different things) may be said to exist to the extent, to the degree, and in the respects in which a society has developed away from the kind of precivilized society which I have been describing. Civilization is, of course, things added to society: cities, writing, public works, the state, the market, and so forth. Another way of looking at it is from the base provided by the folk society. Then we may say that a society is civilized insofar as the community is no longer small, isolated, homogeneous and self-sufficient; as the division of labor is no longer simple; as impersonal relationships come to take the place of personal relationships; as familial connections come to be modified or supplanted by those of political affiliation or contract; and as thinking has become reflective and systematic. I do not mention all of the characteristics of folk societies which I named in foregoing paragraphs; these are enough to suggest the point of view we might adopt. If we do adopt this way of conceiving civilization, we shall think of Toynbee's twenty-one civilizations as different developments away from the folk society. We see then that civilizations do not depart from the nature of the folk society evenly or in the same way. In Chinese civilization the organization of social relationships according to the categories and attitudes of kinship retained its importance while philosophy and the fine arts passed through long histories of development. The Andean civilization developed political and administrative institutions of impressive complexity and far-reaching influence while yet the Indians who developed them were without writing. The Mayan peoples, in contrast, extended their political institutions little beyond that attained by the ordinary tribe while their intellectual specialists carried some parts of mathematics and astronomy to heights that astonish us. In short, the several civilizations start up from their folk bases into specialized developments in which some elements of the folk society are left behind while others are retained. Yet this fact does not destroy the impression that, as a manner of life taken as a whole, civilization is one kind of thing different from the life of the folk society.

The contrast between technical order and moral order helps us to understand the general kind of thing which is civilization. In the folk society the moral order is great and the technical order is small. In primitive and precivilized societies material tools are few and little natural power is used. Neither the formal regulations of the state or church nor the nonmoral ordering of behavior which occurs in the market plays an important part in these societies. It is civilization that develops them.

It is civilization, too, that develops those formal and apparent institutions which both express the moral order and are means toward its realization. The technical order appears not only in tools, power, and an interdependence of people chiefly or wholly impersonal and utilitarian, but also in greater and more varied apparatus for living—apparatus both physical and institutional. Under ten headings Childe [33] has summarized the characteristics of civilized life whether lived at Uruk, Mohenjo-daro, or Uxmal among the Mayans. One, the reappearance of naturalistic art, has a significance not immediately plain, and may be a little doubtful. Of the other nine, six plainly announce the growth of the technical order: (1) the great increase in the size of the settlement (the material equipment for human association becomes far larger); (2) the institution of tribute or taxation with resulting central accumulation of capital; (3) monumental public works; (4) the art of writing; (5) the beginnings of such exact and predictive sciences as arithmetic, geometry, and astronomy; and (6) developed economic institutions making possible a greatly expanded foreign trade. Each of these six suggests the increasing complexity of social organization, and the remaining three criteria explicitly declare features of that social organization which are characteristic of civilization; (7) full-time technical specialists, as in metal working; (8) a privileged ruling class; and (9) the state, or the organization of society on a basis of residence in place of, or on top of, a basis of kinship.

In folk societies the moral order predominates over the technical order. It is not possible, however, simply to reverse this statement and declare that in civilizations the technical order predominates over the moral. In civilization the technical order certainly becomes great. But we cannot truthfully say that in civilization the moral order becomes small. There are ways in civilization in which the moral order takes on new greatness. In civilization the relations between the two orders are varying and complex.

The great transformations of humanity are only in part reported in terms of the revolutions in technology with resulting increases in the number of people living together. There have also occurred changes in the thinking and valuing of men which may also be called "radical and indeed revolutionary innovations." Like changes in the tech-

24

nical order, these changes in the intellectual and moral habits of men become themselves generative of far-reaching changes in the nature of human living. They do not reveal themselves in events as visible and particular as do material inventions, or even always as increasing complexity in the systems of social relationships. Nor is it perhaps possible to associate the moral transformations with limited periods of time as we can associate technological revolutions with particular spans of years. Yet the attempt to identify some of the transformations in men's minds can be made.

One might begin such an attempt by examining the manner of life of the most primitive people we know today, and perhaps also something that is told us about ancient peoples, for evidence of the appearance of forms of thought, belief, or action which a little knowledge of the history of some civilization shows us became influential in changing human life. We see some far-reaching change in the moral or intellectual life of the Western world, perhaps, and so guided we return to the primitive societies to see if it had a beginning there. So we might come to some understanding of some of the relations in history between the two kinds of orders.

As to the trend of this relationship throughout history, I have one general impression. It is that the moral order begins as something pre-eminent but incapable of changing itself, and becomes perhaps less eminent but more independent. In folk society the moral rules bend, but men cannot make them afresh. In civilization the old moral orders suffer, but new states of mind are developed by which the moral order is, to some significant degree, taken in charge. The story of the moral order is attainment of some autonomy through much adversity.

Later Histories

of the Folk Societies

IN THE long view of human affairs, the food-producing revolution and the urban revolution of Childe form into one mighty event: the transformation of the folk society into civilization. The first revolution appears as a prelude and precondition of the second. Taken together, they are one major turning point. Only "the mutation of sub-man into man, which was accomplished in circumstances of which we have no record, was a more profound change." [1] Connecting this second great event, civilization, with the dynamic aspect of existence known to the Chinese as Yang as opposed to Yin, Toynbee remarks that for 98 per cent of all human history mankind reposed on the "ledges" of primitive human nature "before entering on the Yang-like activity of civilization."

From the position we occupy on a higher ledge, looking down on what Toynbee conceives as the dead or apparently paralytic societies remaining or resting on lower ledges, his foremost question is: How did *we* get *here?* The question is as to the genesis of civilization. Toynbee seeks the general circumstances which attend the birth of a civilization, and the characteristic developments in that class of societies which are civilized. From this point of view it is asked to what extent civilizations show recurrences in their developmental phases. To this group of questions different answers have been given by Spengler, Toynbee, Sorokin. The question takes on a multitude of special forms as attention is fixed on particular aspects of the phenomenon of civilization, or is guided by particular interests and hypotheses. The origins of civilization may be seen, as Wittfogel sees them,[2] in the specific necessity to control waters for irrigation and other human use. Or they may be found in a more inclusive and generalized successful response to some sort of challenging difficulty, as Toynbee finds them. The many more special questions as to the origins of civilization may be illustrated by reference to the old problem as to the origins of the state, which some have found in the conquest of one people by another. It is also illustrated in the view that formal law, another aspect of civilization, tends to develop either where there is surplus wealth, unevenly distributed, or where there are major communal enterprises, such as the hunt, war, or public works, requiring regulation.

These great questions are for those who have the scholarly competence which they demand. The enquiry initiated in this chapter starts from the humbler viewpoint of the folk societies themselves. The question here is not, How does civilization come about? but, What becomes of the folk society? Instead of addressing the main outlines of the human adventure from the point of view of civilized men who look back on their beginnings, let us view that adventure from the position of all mankind, originally folk-like in its manner of life, and fairly recently transmuted into societies with new and different manners of life. Here begins a sketchy review of the transformations of the folk societies. Some of these societies have remained on the lower ledges of Professor Toynbee's precipice. How did others come to clamber to higher ledges? What were the influences of civilized peoples upon some of them that caused some precivilized societies to move to different ledges from those they occupied in precivilized times? Toynbee's insights into some of these transmutations are guides in recognizing many of the new forms of human living. Others require new efforts to discern them.

At the time we attempt some account of the transformations of the folk societies, there is not very much left of them. The civilizations of the last five thousand years have destroyed them or have altered them with very small exception. One civilization that developed in Western Europe during very recent times indeed has reached into almost all of even the remote corners where they most successfully persisted in the primary condition. "In this worldwide Western offensive against the rear-guard of the primitive societies, extermination or eviction or subjugation has been the rule and conversion the exception." [3] Most of the folk societies of precivilized times are no more. Such as survive are a mere handful of the population, relative to the immense numbers of the civilized. Anthropology, a product of the Western civilization which, chiefly, has destroyed the folk societies, is the chief agency to bring the survivors to general notice. The anthropologist sees these survivors as marginal to civilization, either because they lie on the outer edges of the continental masses where the civilizations arose (the Australian blackfellow; the Eskimo), or because civilization, swirling around them, leaves them in some relatively inaccessible valley or mountain side (the Vedda of Ceylon; the Ainu; the Cora Indians). [4] In some of the anthropological reports, the surviving folk society is presented as if it were less influenced by civilization than is actually the case at the time of the study; many an ethnological report is something of a reconstruction, a description of the people at the time of their grandfathers, or an account of life at the time of the investigation with the influence of the trader, the mission, or the school somewhat underemphasized. When the purpose of the investigation is to provide the comparative science of society or culture with another independent case to compare, this is proper. In the present connection, however, it is just the kinds of changes that have been brought about in the folk societies that are the center of interest.

With the exception of the few isolated survivors, the rise of the civilizations transformed the precivilized peoples into other kinds of peoples. We may think of civilization as a remaking of man in which the basic type, the folk man, is altered into other types. Some of these types can be recognized as common and perhaps relatively stable. But with later history, the types become so many, so intergraded, and so rapidly changing as to defy analysis.

This remaking of man was the work of the city. As suggested in the first chapter, the archaeology of the Middle East may make it necessary to recognize a period of town life before that of city life. There are sites which suggest that populations intermediate in size between that characterizing the neolithic farming settlement and the ancient city existed in Iraq before Eridu and other cities were distinctly cities. In such towns, says Braidwood, he would suspect that there were administrators, specialists, and an outer clustering of peasants. This is again the question as to the rapidity of acceleration of the curve of that technological development which culminated in city life.

But whether or not we distinguish town from city in this

period, the first important differentiation of societal types took place in these cities and proto-cities. Rather than say each time "town and city," I shall say simply "city." In the city appeared the administrative elite, the literate priest with his opportunities for reflection and cultivation of esoteric knowledge, the specialized artisan, detached from the local community. These are new kinds of men, not only because they have found new kinds of economic support, but because, in the greater impersonality of their relations with others and in their relative independence of the village community with its local culture and "inward-facingness," these city men have a new world view and essential style of life.

The developing city required economic support from a wider and wider area of production, and so affected, at first only in terms of labor, tribute, and sale, peoples as yet not civilized, or only partly civilized. The process of differentiation of societal types took place also outside of the city, by extension of its influence on folk societies. I suppose that a Sumerian city, or an Egyptian kingdom, drew its supplies from peoples in all kinds and degrees of transformation of their style of life, from more remote peoples still primitive and tribal to the city-dominated farmers at their very gates. And the early city extends its influence by procreation of other cities: Byblos, in Syria, becomes a semi-Egyptian city; after Assyrian merchants have settled in Cappadocia, a variant of Mesopotamian civilization develops there.[5] So secondary centers of urban influence came into being. This process of transformation of folk peoples into urban peoples or partly urbanized peoples has never ceased. It continues today on the Western-managed tropical plantation, in the African kraal, the

American Indian reservation, the Macedonian village, and the Ozark mountain valley.

Our historians of the ancient civilizations, when they come to describe cities so old and highly developed as stood in Egypt or in Mesopotamia in the third millennium before Christ, use the word "peasant" for those peoples close at hand whose labors made the city possible. The word points to a human type. Rather than use it, as some have,[6] for any community of small-scale producers for market, let us reserve it for this new type. It required the city to bring it into existence. There were no peasants before the first cities. And those surviving primitive peoples who do not live in terms of the city are not peasants. The Siriono Indians are not peasants; nor are the Navaho. But it is possible positively to characterize those peoples who are.

The peasant, like the primitive tribesman, is indigenous. He lives where he has always lived, and the city has grown up out of a kind of life which, in fundamental custom and belief, is his too. Perhaps its influence came to him from near at hand, and he has walked to the city to sell his produce or to contribute his labor; or perhaps the nearest city is so far away that its influence has reached him only after long delay. But in either case he is long used to the existence of the city, and its ways are, in altered form, part of his ways. The peasant is a rural native whose long established order of life takes important account of the city.

The account that the peasant takes of the city or town is economic, political, and moral. The peasant has some product which the city consumes, and there are products of the city—metal tools, guns, patent medicines, or electric flashlights—which the peasant takes from the manufacturers in the city. Since the coming of money into the world, the peasant village has come in great degree to define its economic affairs in terms of this measure. In Oriental peasant villages the extraordinary expenditures required by the marriage of a child or the advent of a festival are met by co-operative credit associations, "a mechanism for collective saving and lending," [7] and these institutions function in terms of money. They exist in villages in China,[8] in Japan,[9] and in India.[10]

The relations between peasant and town or city are expressed in part in financial institutions. Gain is calculated; some crop or other product is sold, in the village or elsewhere, to a buyer of a more urbanized community who pays in money. Taxation is also present; when tribute is regularized into taxation, a tribal people is on the way to becoming peasantry. In certain East Indian villages the accountant is an important specialist.[11] In the Chinese villages described by Fei,[12] the peasant requires the assistance of townsman or city man to finance his agriculture. A town collector of rice sends an "agent boat" to the villages; the agent gets the townsman collector to lend rice to the peasant when the peasant has no more; the agent guarantees the return of the rice to the townsman by the peasant when his new rice comes to market. Or village people borrow money from wealthy people in the towns with whom they have connections; the rate of interest is very high. In East Indian villages the moneylenders that interested Henry Maine when he wrote of Indian village life eighty years ago [13] still flourish; recently their operations have come to be regulated by modern law; they still function "and in a highly sophisticated way; they generally cover vast areas, working in teams and visiting their fixed villages along the bus and rail lines at least twice a year; they establish credit ratings by systematic interviewing and by taking help

from local agent-spies." [14] Pawnbrokers in the towns probably account for a significant part of the village credit in
India.[15] We may summarize the economic character of
the peasant village by saying that it combines the primitive
brotherhood of the precivilized folk community with the
economic nexus characteristic of civilized society. So far
as the peasant community faces inward, the relationships that compose it are still personal and familial, but
now they are modified by a spirit of pecuniary advantage.

This pecuniary spirit contributes to the formation of an
added dimension of the peasant's social life: in the peace-
ful and stable relationships with outsiders. The peasant
village maintains its local solidarity, its folklike inward-
facingness, but now qualifies the sharp exclusiveness of the
primitive settlement with institutionalized forms for ad-
mitting strangers. In the idealized typical folk society all
members of one's own community are kinsmen; all others
are enemies. In some real primitive societies, under original
conditions of isolation, this condition is approximated; we
remember Professor A. R. Radcliffe-Brown's account of
how, to gain admittance to a settlement of unfamiliar aborigines, this anthropologist's guide had first to establish, by
that dialectic of the kinship term so important there, his
connection by kinship with the group into which admission
was sought.[16] But in the peasant village there is institutionalized provision for the stranger. When he is a specialist in the business, the East Indian moneylender is in the
village by right and necessity, but he is not of it. The village fathers discuss their problems without him. The simple
agriculturalist will be admitted fully into the moral life of
the community. But for him to be admitted there may be
some ritual of acceptance, of adoption. In some villages a

settler may be admitted as a "soil brother." Such persons are admitted at par. They become like the native born.

But the admission of one who will not become a full participant in the local life, but will merely live there and serve it in a specialized and instrumental capacity, is a more serious matter. I was present in a village of Mayan Mexican peasants when the question was debated as to whether a certain traveling vendor of city goods and buyer of locally produced swine should be allowed, on his petition, to settle in the village and open a store. The villagers had themselves already established small stores in which to sell city products they themselves imported. The admission to the community, however, of one who would not be a farmer like themselves and who would presumably have no part in the religious and moral life with which the agriculture was bound up, was a momentous step, and they took it only after due consideration. The institutionalized resident stranger is a feature of peasant life. At any earlier stage of that process whereby the tribal community becomes a peasant community, the question may be as to the admission of traveling vendors from the outside, who are not even allowed to pass a night in the settlement. So, among the more primitive Maya of Quintana Roo, Villa, my associate ethnologist, had to appear as a traveling peddler of cloth, medicine, and gunpowder as a first step in getting permission to reside for a season among them. With established peasantry, however, the traveling merchant, the caravan trade, the permanent store kept by Arab, or Syrian, or Chinese, or urbanite from Tyre or Sidon, come to be familiar.

The economic interdependence of peasant village and city finds political expression in institutions for control of the local community by power exerted from the city. The

34

established relations of the peasant village with the urban world are political as well as economic. Where the local community is still more or less tribal, the urban control may be exercised through punitive expeditions, actual or threatened, but when peasantry are fully present, the secular and impersonal control of the city is continuous and precise. The representative of the central power may be someone derived from the village itself, as when the literate Chinese villager who has passed an examination deals on behalf of the village with the bureaucrats in the yamen. Or the village leaders, the panchayat, or the elders of the mir, will deal with the outside power in ways to which they have become adjusted. These varying forms of political adjustment to the central power come into being whether the central power is a city-state, a kingdom, or an empire. The peasantry of feudalism have their own patterns of political relationship to power that is above them, although in this case the influence of the city appears in the manor and ruling elite, even in the immediate absence of the city itself.

This relatively stable relationship between peasant and city is in part shaped by the cultural advances of the city and the incorporation into the peasant life of institutions developed in the course of this advance. Entertainment is one form of city-born activity. In the precivilized society the dramatic and lyric arts are inseparable from the religion or from the mythic content of the local culture, and secular professional entertainment is unknown. This is a creature of the city. Peasants look in part to town or city for their entertainment; the conditions of peace and relative freedom of movement make it possible for traveling entertainers to come to the peasant villages, entertainers whose models are in part urban. The migratory professional entertainers of medieval Europe are well known. Writing of East Indian villages, Altekar tells us how the agricultural labors of the villagers are interrupted by traveling singers and dancers.[17] In China dramatic performances entertain the villagers; the companies may consist of amateurs organized locally, or they may be made up of more professional players who travel from community to community.[18] The Mexican peasant at festivals receives musicians employed from a town, or is amused by a traveling circus. The festival is better, the prestige of the village is the higher, if the musicians hired come from a more urbanized town.

The peasant is also adjusted, in ways that characterize his style of life, to that outstanding feature of civilization, writing. The precivilized hunter or villager is preliterate; the peasant is illiterate. The existence of the art of writing has become an element in his mode of life, although he himself perhaps cannot read or write. He must take account of those who can, and things written are meaningful objects in his life. The sociology of literacy has not yet been written. But it should be possible to recognize the characteristic forms of adjustment to literacy. It may be too much to say that in the ancient civilizations writing remained "a mystery, a specialized profession too abstruse to combine with manual avocations"; [19] some of the earliest uses of writing were in connection with purposes apparently exoteric and secular. But it is probably correct to say that in the early civilizations of the Old World, as among the Maya of the New, there developed a higher learning dependent on literacy; and the literate specialists, in many cases priestly in function, were not also artisans. The literate man tended to become, until modern times, a kind of

36

professional. In many a peasant village literacy is confined to the few, and these few use their knowledge either to communicate what is held in sacred books—traditional writings of moral and religious force—or to communicate with the city world in secular matters. In the villages of Quintana Roo, among Indians not yet become peasants, the art of literacy at the time when Alfonso Villa Rojas studied these people was entrusted in each sub-tribe to only two individuals, who passed on the esoteric art to successor-acolytes. The art was used to read certain sacred writings treasured by the tribe, or to read communications from God conveniently reduced to writing.[20] In the fully developed Mayan peasant village we found the use of literacy as the sacred specialists' medium of communication with tradition to be represented by certain specialists who knew how to read traditional prayers. But there literacy had come also to have secular significance. Certain men learned to read in order to understand written communications from the town or city, and to keep the records and accounts necessitated by the economic and political relationships with the city.[21] Finally, in the villages stimulated to that effort by urban leaders, these Yucatecan peasants began to undertake the extension of literacy to everyone. But it was noticeable then how greatly the motivation of the villager lay in matters of status. The townsman's ways were looked up to, and the townsman was literate; therefore the peasant wished to learn to read. Yet the view persisted that insofar as literacy was a practical necessity, it was enough that somebody in the village should be literate. Today, when men plan to make all the world's peoples literate, the attempts to do so encounter, among other difficulties, the limited motivations of the peasant. Nor is it clear that universal literacy would of itself change the peasant style of life. Where the uses of literacy are limited, the localism and traditionalism of the village is not much affected.

Much of what I have said about the peasant life can be related to the fact that in his case, as contrasted with that of the precivilized hunter or agriculturalist, city people or townspeople are included in his system of relationships of status. The tribesman or dweller in a precivilized band or hamlet looks across at other such people to whom he does not accord a special status within his own plan of life. To precivilized man the outsider is, perhaps, useful, different, hostile, dangerous, amusing, contemptible. But the peasant knows himself as a part of a moral world in which the city man is also included. The city man expresses certain values, as of material success, or religious authority, or special access to the meaning of life, which he, the peasant, also cares about. Peasant and urbanite are, in certain things, one society, and the peasant knows it. It does not follow that the peasant looks upward to the city man in everything. Indeed, among such peasants as I have known or have read about, there is characteristically present the attitude that in certain important moral qualities, as for example industry, physical endurance, honesty, and sexual morality, the peasant is superior.

Undeterred by Sorokin's conclusion [22] that there is little evidence of a typical rural mind, E. K. L. Francis has turned to the specifically peasant form of life, and, through a study of Hesiod's *Works and Days,* has attempted a characterization of the Boeotian peasant of that time which might stand for all peasantry.[23] Francis seeks the personality type of the peasant, or the peasant's "integrated pattern of dominant attitudes"—his style of life. In Hesiod's pages, Francis finds a pattern of dominant attitudes emphasizing a practical and utilitarian attitude toward nature, yet with such a positive valuation of work as sees it as not only materially productive but also a fulfillment of divine command; a de-emphasis of emotion; a concern with security rather than adventure; a high valuation of procreation and children; a desire for wealth; and the joining of social justice with work as basic ethical notions. The type of thought and feeling which emerges seems to me readily applicable, for the most part, to the Polish peasant as made known to us in both science [24] and literature,[25] to the Chinese peasant insofar as I know about him, to the Kurdish peasant as Braidwood knows him, and to the Mayan Indian and Guatemalan Hispanic peasants with whom I have direct acquaintance. If there is such a peasant style of life, the comparison of it with that of pastoral warrior nomads, already attempted,[26] might be developed.

The peasant appears as a human type that is recognizable, widespread, and long enduring, brought about by the development of civilization. Presumably it is such a mode of existence as permits continuation of many of the adaptive characteristics of the folk society with the new necessities brought about by the city. The peasant society exists by virtue of the traditional moral solidarity to be found in any isolated folk society; kinship relationships are still of first importance; the ends of living are implicit and strongly felt. On the other hand the peasant makes certain elements of civilization a part of his life: a trading spirit, money, formal and impersonal controls, whether economic or political. In many peasant communities the division of labor has produced many kinds of specialists. The peasant community has developed in very important respects indeed away from the ideal type of folk society. The peasant style of life is a balanced adjustment between moral order and technical order. It is, probably, a form of living which is adaptive in periods and places where the influence of the city has spread, but not very rapidly, into precivilized communities. The necessary condition of peasant life is that the system of values of the peasant be consistent, in the main, with those of the city people who constitute, so to speak, its other dimension of existence. Peasants "constitute part-societies with part-cultures." [27] Writing of the Russian gentry at the turn of the nineteenth century, Henri Troyat says that in spite of serfdom and the French education of these gentry, "their faith, their tastes, their essential fears and hopes were the same (although they little suspected it) as those of the common people whose ignorance they sneered at." [28]

With these thoughts to guide us, we may speculate as to the origins of the peasantry out of precivilized folk. We may imagine that not all precivilized peoples were characterized by systems of values amenable to a peasant life. The values of the uncivilized Comanche would have to undergo very great change to suit a peasant condition. Some precivilized people were probably more inclined than others to fill the role of peasantry. Even among neighboring communities of Melanesian gardeners we are told that there are great differences as to the values emphasized. Presumably among the precivilized Asiatics and Europeans there were similar differences. Some of these were perhaps already more practically disposed toward nature, already sober and unemotional in emphasis. Yet we know that the ethical system of a people—at least of a civilized people— can undergo marked change in not a great many generations; the case of England in the last three hundred years is commonly cited. At any rate, the introduction of agriculture presumably bent the ethical system of many people who became farmers into ways of thought and feeling that were congenial to peasantry. The development of the market and the coming of the city completed the transformation.

In the historic processes whereby the folk societies were transformed, we may distinguish a primary phase in which the transformations were local and within a single cultural tradition, from that much more complex secondary phase in which peoples of widely differing traditions and cultures were brought into contact, modified and uprooted. In a published map of the distribution of civilization about 3000 B.C.,[29] the civilized areas of the world appear as "three tiny patches of the earth's surface." [30]

At this time only the primary phase in the transformation of the folk societies had occurred. Some of the agriculturalists near the new cities had become peasants. Within the new cities new kinds of men were coming into being: the administrative and power-holding elite, the literati, certain kinds of artisans detached from rural local communities. Farther away from the cities more remote peoples had acquired products and inventions of the cities without losing their essential independence of the city, without becoming peasants. The peasants then in existence were peasants on the main line, so to speak; their descendants are familiar to us in Asia, the Middle East, Eastern Europe. But in the later phase, at the periphery of civilizational expanse, other kinds of peasants came into existence, especially in Latin America. In this latter case the folk peoples that became peasants had cultures very different from those who, beginning as their conquerors, came to be the ruling elite of the folk now transformed into peasantry. But here the transformation required the adjustment of the indigenous Indian folk to a way of life consistent with that of their Spanish or Portuguese conquerors. The Latin American Indian begins as a member of a morally independent folk society whose people look across at invader and conqueror; he becomes a peasant, looking up —and down—toward a ruling class. All stages of the process of transformation of tribal folk into peasantry culturally homogeneous with their urban elite are to be observed in Latin America.

Of the types of men brought about within the city itself, I say little, for lack of knowledge of ancient history. In Harper's translation of the Code of Hammurabi, I see mentioned a great many different kinds of the specialists that existed in Babylon—freemen and slaves, landlords and tenants, agents and merchants, winesellers, priestesses, physicians, veterinaries, boatmen, herdmen, brickmakers, tailors, and carriers. And in the city appeared social classes, not merely people differing in prestige and power while identical in culture (as the social classes of the Kwakiutl Indians), nor classes represented by the difference between invading conqueror and invaded native people, but social classes in conscious protest against their contrasting positions in what Max Weber calls "life chances." And the specialization of function within the ruling elite of the city provided special types of men within that more inclusive group. The typical functions developed by those specialists in reading and writing who appear in civilization, the styles of life that come to be developed out of these functions, and the characteristic positions occupied by the literate in the new civilization and in its contacts with other peoples, less or differently civilized, may some day be described in a future sociology of civilizational types.

In emphasizing two contrasting aspects of the functions and roles of the literate in the early and later civilizations,

Childe and Toynbee point to a difference that might deserve the distinguishing terms that these writers give to the two kinds of literate people. Childe [31] is impressed with the separation between craftsmanship and literacy in the early civilizations, and with the "scholastic attitude" developed by those clerks who used writing to set down traditional lore and knowledge and who came to develop the exact sciences and philosophy. Some of these became custodians and interpreters of sacred books. In this aspect of their functions, internal to the developing civilization, we might speak of the new type of men as the literati. The literate elite of old China illustrate the type. These persons are enclosed within the culture that has become civilization. They carry it forward into a more systematic and reflective phase. Called into being by a revolution in the technology, they are themselves to become the agents of distant transformations of the moral life.

Toynbee,[32] on the other hand, writes of the functions of those literate persons who mediate between the society out of which they arose and some other and alien civilization which is impinging upon it. These people have learned something alien to the culture of their native community; they "have learnt the tricks of the intrusive civilization's trade so far as may be necessary to enable their own community, through their agency, just to hold its own in a social environment in which life is ceasing to be lived in accordance with the local tradition and is coming more and more to be lived in the style imposed by the intrusive civilization upon the aliens who fall under its dominion." [33] Such are the Oriental diplomatists who learn to deal with Westerners, "the civil servant who has picked up the practice of conducting the public administration according to Western forms," and so forth. We may add the educated African or the American Indian with a literate knowledge of the white man and his ways. These people Toynbee calls by the word which developed for them in Russia, the intelligentsia. In contrast to the literati, the member of the intelligentsia "is born to be unhappy." He belongs to two worlds, not one; he is a "marginal man." [34] In the Mayan village of peasants which I knew best, some years ago, the literati were represented by the *maestros cantores* reading and interpreting the sacred prayers; the intelligentsia were appearing in those men who learned the ways and the writing of the city world the better to deal with it. The former used literacy to carry on the local sacred tradition; the latter used it to admit the ways of the world outside. But at this early stage of differentiation of literate types, the two tendencies may appear in the same individual.[35]

This mention of the intelligentsia, like the reference to the formation of peasants through conquest of folk peoples by alien civilizations, has carried the story of the transformation of the folk societies into the second phase, in which the expanding civilization reaches out to folk societies with cultures different in traditional content from those which gave rise to that civilization. By the diffusion of elements of civilization to peripheral peoples there resulted, of course, changes in the modes of life of such peoples; the story is familiar in the effects of Mediterranean civilization upon peoples north of these centers. Here we may try to think of the effects of the expansion, not as diffusion of civilization, but as the production of distinguishable social types.

We start again from the politically and morally independent folk society. The expansion of civilization in some cases pushed up to such societies, or flowed around them, leaving them politically and morally independent. The

Lolos on the Chinese frontier, or certain American Indians not yet put on reservations, illustrate this situation. These became enclaved folk. In some cases, as illustrated by the Hopi Indians, the political independence may be partly lost while the moral independence is largely maintained. Or the folk society may be taken into the society of the invading civilization, as a partner, yet retaining for a long time its cultural distinctness. This is apparently an uncommon outcome. Toynbee [36] mentions three such cases: the Scottish Highlanders, the Maoris of New Zealand, the Araucanians of Chile. Such peoples are more than mere enclaves; they are minority peoples; they make an adjustment which retains their own traditional moral order in considerable degree while yet they take part in the engulfing society. A commoner and not entirely different outcome is represented by the imperialized folk, if so we may call the many folklike peoples who came to be dominated by either the political rule or the economic exploitation of an invading civilization. In most of these cases the old moral order of the folk is thrown into confusion, and gives way; it may not do so for some time, however. The Indonesians working on the Dutch plantations, described by Boeke,[37] illustrate such a people. There are many such in Africa today as well.

In the long run, however, the folkways of most of these peoples are transformed into a manner of life which approximates that of the invader. If such peoples are not early destroyed, by force, or by such disorganization as breaks down the will to live,[38] they are assimilated. On the other hand, invasion and conquest commonly stimulate a reaction in which local culture is reorganized. These reactions, restorations of moral order, receive some attention in the next chapter. One such might be mentioned in the present connection. In the process of accommodation and assimilation to the ways of the white man, surviving American Indian groups have come to know one another, and especially to know the "Indianness" of each other. Moreover, they have responded similarly to the expectations of the white man as to how Indians should dress, act, dance. So Indian peoples have become conscious of respects in which they are alike and different from white people, and have come also to assume the role which white people tend to expect of all Indians, whatever their original customary life. Dances, rituals, and other elements of culture have been passed about among Indian groups, now in closer association with one another than was true under aboriginal conditions. There is coming about a sort of generalized American native folk. Today the generalized Indian is almost one minority people. Pan-Indianism is both a culture and a cause. One imagines that a similar development might later take place in Africa; it begins already, at least in West Africa.

The foregoing has been written as if the separate isolated folk societies merely remain where they are and are transformed *in situ*, as the archaeologist says. But this is not the case. The expansion of civilization results in vast and complex migrations of peoples. The effects of these movements upon the transformation of the civilizations themselves constitute a great theme in Toynbee's study of history. Here, in continuing this rough typological account of the transformation of the folk societies, I mention aspects of these effects on the periphery of the civilizations, from the point of view of the folk societies themselves. And the changes in the moral order that Toynbee discusses are highly instructive to me when I try to consider the later relations between technical and moral order.

The expanding civilization may in cases remove whole populations of folk peoples and set them down in some distant land. Occasionally the transplantation may be accomplished in such a way as to establish in the new home enough representatives of the folk society so that the indigenous culture may resume its life in the new land. The Bush Negroes of Dutch Guiana [39] approximate such a condition. The Arizona Yaqui suggest it; [40] they are a transplanted folk. The causes of the migration of the ancestors of the Gypsies from their home in India is unknown. But the outcome has been an oddity: a world-nomad folk. "They certainly have an ethos all their own." [41] They have adopted vagrancy as a style of life. When the folk are removed in such a way as to mingle in the new land of people of notably different languages and cultures, and are thrown down in conditions of isolation, they make a new folk life, but now chiefly out of elements of living provided by their conquerors. The plantation Negroes of America are remade folk. The process of making folk is not something that went on once only before the advent of the civilizations. To a degree it continues wherever the conditions of isolation exist. One of the things learned in the course of a study of culture in the Yucatan peninsula [42] was that these Indian peoples who, having been peasantlike serfs on plantations, retired into the bush after their unsuccessful war against the white conqueror became in a century of chosen isolation more folklike than they had been. The folk culture that continued to develop in the bush was made up of more European than of Indian elements. Yet in the integration of custom and institution, in the presence of strong implicit conceptions of the purpose of life, the manner of life grew more folklike, not less. So too we recognize in the development of folklore, and a certain style of life, that isolated occupational groups from civilized communities represent, in some aspects, the process of formation of folk. Lumbermen, cowboys, river boatmen are quasi folk. And the resemblances of the isolated sectarian communities to the folk societies is a familiar fact.

We seem to see, in the varying transformations of the primary folkness of mankind, the effects of opposing tendencies in the construction and stability of the moral order. It may be repeated that the folk society is that society in which the technical order is subordinated within the moral order. The moral order is there, self-consistent and strong. As the technical order develops with the food-producing and urban revolutions, as the civilizations produce within themselves a differentiation of human types, and as they also reach out to affect distant peoples, there is a double tendency within the moral order. On the one hand, the old moral orders are shaken, perhaps destroyed. On the other, there is a rebuilding of moral orders on new levels. The rebuilding may be within the peripheral local community, as in the case of freshly isolated Indians of the forests of Quintana Roo, or among isolated American Negroes. Or the rebuilding may occur so as to include more and different peoples, who have been brought into some kind of relationship already by the expansions of the technical order. The moral order grows by death and rebirth. Or, to change the figure, within the life of the moral order of mankind there is a perpetual anabolism and catabolism.

The coming of the civilizations disturbed, probably forever, the primordial relation between these tendencies. Then the technical order underwent such an acceleration as to throw the ancient moral orders into profound confusion. The civilizations brought many kinds of different peoples together. We read of archaeological evidence for an Indian cult celebrated in a Sumerian city.[43] There were Egyptian foreign colonies in Syrian cities.[44] Heterogeneity is the first characteristic of the city, ancient or modern. And with heterogeneity come doubts as to the moral order. Civilization is deracination. Within the city the roots are torn through the heterogeneity of populations, the exploitation of minorities, the specialization of knowledge and function. On the edges of expanding civilizations the civilization meets with people of whom it makes half-converts to the city way of life, or whom it employs as mercenaries, seizes as slaves, or sends as merchants to distant lands. Now, telling our lesser story from the bottom up, we have met with those kinds of peoples whom Toynbee calls —in an unusual extension of meaning—"the proletariats." [45] These are in part within the civilization itself, the "internal proletariat." This proletariat is made up, he tells us, "of the disinherited and uprooted members of the society's own body social; partially disinherited members of alien civilizations and primitive societies that were conquered and exploited without being torn up by the roots; and doubly disinherited conscripts from these subject populations who were not only uprooted but were also enslaved and deported in order to be worked to death on distant plantations.[46] These words refer to the internal proletariat of the Hellenic civilization; other proletariats Toynbee finds to be similar. The "external proletariats" are composed of peoples marginal to a civilization, who have ceased to follow the cultural leadership of the civilization and have turned against it, using, in the violent form of the response, the new instruments of the technical order of the civilization. "The surrounding primitive peoples are no longer charmed but are repelled." [47] They cease a disposition to enter a moral order of a civilization whose. moral

49

order is not simple and compelling, and react against that civilization. Here the anthropologist thinks of one of the many groups of whom Toynbee thinks in conceiving the external proletariat, partly civilized American Indian peoples on the American frontier, acting either as warriors against the whites, or as creators of new nativistic religions.

The point about Toynbee's proletarians in our present connection is that they have ceased to live within the ambit of their ancient moral orders. "The true hallmark of the proletarian is . . . a consciousness—and the resentment that this consciousness inspires—of being disinherited from his ancestral place in society." [48] The reaction Toynbee finds may be an explosion of savagery, or it may take the form of a religious movement. The proletarian is a product of the city, of civilization. What is new about him is that he is aware of the blow dealt to his moral order, and reacts to this awareness. With civilization the problems of the moral order move to a new level of struggle and achievement. It is the level marked by self-consciousness, of sense of deprivation, and of conscious creativeness.

Internal growth, and the effects of the meeting of peoples, are two aspects of the whole of cultural development that are ever of interest to anthropologists. These two played their parts in the transformations of the folk societies. Of the many folk peoples that existed in many parts of the earth five to ten thousand years ago, a few, already provided with granaries or with food animals, built themselves cities and so made a style of life new to humanity. This style of life was characterized by a development and complexity of the technical order theretofore unknown. And it was characterized by both disorganization and regrowth of the moral order. While the literati were using reading and writing to transmute the old sacred tradition of the folk into science and philosophy, the old tradition was being broken down under the influence of commerce, specialization of useful function, and the movements and mixings of peoples. The style of life of the city included doubt and dissent, and ultimately the displacement and dissatisfactions of those new and city-made kinds of peoples, the proletariats. Meanwhile, as the civilizations moved outward to meet peoples still tribal and folklike, they slowly transformed the country people nearest at hand into peasantry. Farther away, the city men dealt with tribesmen and rulers of barbarian states, and here still other styles of life came into being: folk enclaved within civilization, policed or protected, and yet retaining the moral predominance of folk life; peoples subordinated to the rule of the city men or in long continuing warfare with them; peoples transplanted by their captors to new lands, there in ignorance and isolation again to become folk, perhaps to be taken into the technical and moral orders of their conquerors, or perhaps, in the discovery of the preciousness of the ancient tradition which they were losing, creating, out of the very anguish of their loss, a new cult, a new sense of the separateness and importance of their style of life.

The phrase "style of life" has come into this discussion to meet the need for a term that will suggest what is most fundamental and enduring about the ways of a group persisting in history. "Ethos," "basic culture patterns," "values," "configuration of culture," and "modal personality" are other terms which have arisen among anthropologists in response to this need. If "culture" itself does not seem to meet the need, it is because that word may suggest too

51

narrowly the items of institutions and belief which go to make up the anthropologist's account of, say, the Hopi Indians as contrasted with the Navaho Indians.

"Style of life," as used here, includes the ways of getting a living insofar as these contribute to the shaping of ideas of the good life. The term emphasizes the judgments, implicit or expressed, as to what right conduct is. And not excluded are the lesser tastes and preferences that give to a people its characteristic flavor, so to speak. When Lionel Trilling writes of *manners,* as "a culture's hum and buzz of implication . . . half-uttered or unuttered or unutterable expressions of value," [49] he is thinking of the style of life.

The phrase has a usefulness here; it need not be continued. Better than "culture," "style of life" admits the possibility that people with very different specific contents of culture may have very similar views of the good life. As the anthropologist would ordinarily put it, the cultures of the Lapp and of the Bedouin are very different. These two peoples are differently fed and housed; they have different religions, customs, and institutions. Nevertheless it may prove to be true that in certain general ways of looking upon the world, in the emphasis on certain virtues and ideals, in certain manners of independence and hospitality natural to a free-roaming people, Lapp and Bedouin have the same style of life. But "style of life," like "culture," does imply some harmony of parts and some continuity through time, the generations looking backward to their own lives in the past and again to their own lives in the future. Toynbee's internal proletariats are for a time without style of life. The disinherited who followed Spartacus as he raged up and down the Italian peninsula were then without style of life. But a shepherd on the hills of Galilee has a style of life; so has a Hopi Indian; so too had an aristocrat of the *ancien régime*.

And extending the term to forms of human existence still more general, one might say that folk life, in contrast to civilized life, is one style of life, in spite of the very great specific cultural differences among precivilized or primitive societies. Peasantry then, whether Mexican or Chinese or Polish, is that style of life which prevailed outside of the cities and yet within their influence during the long period between the urban revolution and the industrial revolution. The specific styles of life which civilization creates are beyond my powers to discern and distinguish. On the outskirts of American cities at least two kinds of people with two distinct styles of life are to be found living together physically but separate morally: rural farmers and suburbanites. In the cities themselves ways of living develop in which the continuity from generation to generation is impaired or almost lost. If continuity is lost, if people see no clear lines for the development of their careers, certainly not for their children's careers, do we still speak of a style of life? What sort of style of life is "other-directedness"? [50] In modern civilization the making of new forms of man takes new turns, which may demand new terms for their description.

◇◇◇

III

Civilization

and the Moral Order

DURING that long period of human history when there were no cities, the relations between one folk society and another did not often involve, we may safely assume, the conscious struggle of an ethical system to maintain itself. If today we look at the attitudes that prevail as between two primitive peoples, each with its own settlement or territory, we see a sense of superiority and perhaps of hostility. But we do not see a fear of moral assault. The people of one band or tribe regard their own way of life as better than that of other people, and may even attribute humanity to themselves alone: other people are seen as something less than perfect men. "The Negroes (of the Ituri forest) distinguish four ranks or orders of living beings: people, pygmies, chimpanzees, and other animals." [1] Primitive men may seize horses or take heads from a different and neighboring group. But the people of such a folk society are not then engaged in a conscious struggle for moral dominance or for the survival of a traditional ethical system. The Cheyenne Indian hated the Crow Indian as an enemy to engage in physical encounter, not moral encounter.

It may, however, have happened, as it has happened in historical times, that one folk society conquered another, or that a folk people of one tradition and group consciousness came to settle, for one reason or another, among a people of a different tradition and group consciousness. Insofar as this happened before the rise of cities, it presumably did give rise to the fear of loss of one's own way of life. We must entertain the idea of such exceptional situations in which there developed a conscious struggle to protect a threatened moral order. But, even so, again to judge by such cases as are known to us from recent times, the threatened community did no more than to shut itself away from the other community. For two and a half centuries a community of Tewa Indians has lived among the Hopi of First Mesa. They maintain their cultural integrity. Marriage with the Hopi was for long prohibited; the Tewa never speak the Hopi language though some know it; Tewa ceremonies are kept secret from the Hopi; a myth of an ancient curse sanctifies the cultural separation.[2] But we do not read that Tewa and Hopi send missionaries to each other. It is not possible rightly to suppose that the precivilized age was distinguished by the important presence of missionary or prophet. The preacher of conversion and the preacher of moral regeneration are creatures of civilization. It is through the city that the many moral orders confined to small local communities become something to be defended, struggled for, remade.

It is the city that makes world-wide and conspicuous the self-conscious struggle to maintain a traditional ethos, as it is in the city, in the first place, that traditional morality is attacked and broken down. The conflict on the religious or ethical level between city and country, urbanite and peasant, sophisticated mind and simple villager or tribesman, is an ancient and familiar theme. It is known to us from history and from ethnology. In the Maya village of Chan Kom, to which my mind ever reverts in these connections, my good friend, a certain thoughtful villager, saw with dismay the coming of the highway that would bring the evils of the city to the peasant community his own leadership had built. Recoiling from the consequences he had not foreseen of an urbanization for which he had put forth great effort, he began to view the city as a source of moral evil. "With the road will come drunkenness, idleness, vice," he said. So, too, after David had made Jerusalem the Israelite capital, and after Solomon had caused the city to flourish, the prophets in the hinterland inveighed against the idleness and corruption of the city. A herdsman peasant, Amos, cried: "Shall a trumpet be blown in the city, and the people not be afraid?" and he heard the Lord say: "I abhor the excellency of Jacob, and hate his palaces: therefore will I deliver up the city with all that is therein." [3] The Rechabite movement in Israel was a movement to return to the "good old days" of rustic simplicity. Deny civilization, and ye shall be saved. Hosea looked forward to a time when Israel should again live in tents. In the seventh chapter of the Book of Isaiah we read the words of a prophet who thought that the good life would come again if the land should return to wilderness and the inhabitants again take to hunting. In the store-front church and the sand-lot tent of the modern American city we find today the little prophets of rural revolt against the moral threat of the city. And the enduring conflict between rural piety and urban rational wickedness was dramatized for those of us old enough to remember the day when Bryan and Darrow faced each other in Dayton, Tennessee.

We do not have to adopt all of Spengler's views in which

urban civilization is seen as moribund culture, and in which the country gentleman is held up as the supreme human type, to accept his assertion that "world-city and province are the basic ideas of every civilization." [4] The relations between city people and country people form a major separation, a principal frontier of human relations. This, a fact not easily observed by the archaeologist, is one consequence of the urban revolution. There are now city people, a new kind of people, "traditionless, utterly matter of fact, religionless, clever, unfruitful, deeply contemptuous of the countryman." [5] And there are now provincials, people whose character is determined by their relations with the city. These relations are ethical; in the provinces as within the city itself traditional values are doubted, defended, attacked, and perhaps restored. Henceforth there is at best an uneasy peace on the moral frontier between city and country. The peasant has made a workable adjustment; he is within civilization, but he is wary; he would rather keep the city at a distance. The disorganized or uprooted barbarians on the military frontier, the "external proletariat," have felt the sword of the city turn in the soul as well as in the body; their way of life is threatened, and they would defend it.

Thus it seems that the influence of the city on the folk society, and on societies that have passed through some part or aspect of the transformation from folk to urban society, has produced and continues to produce forms of disorganization and reorganization of the moral order that might prove susceptible to generalization. The double process of tearing down and building up the moral order which may be recognized in the history of the influence of civilization on the folk societies, appears within limits and in types that can perhaps some day be recognized. If a

57

society is left alone, the anabolic process predominates, and the moral order develops toward consistency and paramountcy; enter the invader in person or by his tools and his teaching, and the moral order is thrown into confusion. But with another period of relative isolation and stability, the moral order, altered in content and perhaps in scope, is re-established.

Such a study of the natural history of the moral order is far beyond my competence. It may be barely suggested here in terms of a series of changes in the society of the Yucatec Maya. I shall draw on information that Alfonso Villa and I gathered about events that occurred in the histories of three or four communities in Yucatan or Quintana Roo, and on some of the published studies made by the students of Maya civilization before and just after the coming of the Spaniards. For all the early period the facts we want to know are mostly lacking, so this will be a brief and shadowy story. With what appears below as to the conditions of moral order in communities of Yucatan will be included some references to conditions in the society of ancient Rome, as these seem to me comparable. I should make it quite plain that I have not studied ancient Rome. These are impressions received from reading the pages of Fowler,[6] Bailey,[7] and Halliday.[8] These impressions are included so as to suggest a resemblance in the history of the moral order between peoples of different epochs and traditions.

The first Maya cities were built between 500 B.C. and 300 A.D. The uncertainty depends upon alternative readings of the earliest dates we have written in the Indian hieroglyph, and on the possibility that future archaeology may uncover cities earlier than the ones we now know in ruined form. These ancient Maya cities were cities in that they were centers of control of rural people dependent upon them, and in that in them dwelt literati who carried a folk tradition into a specialized, esoteric, and reflective form. Although all ancient cities were presumably alike in that they brought about a distinction between dependent folk people and some new kinds of urban people, the kinds of cities and the kinds of urban people developed differed as each civilization differed from others. The commerce that was found in early Mesopotamian cities was probably not present, in significant degree, in the ancient Maya city. Nor was the Maya city, if we may be allowed to call it that, a place of residence of common people. It lacked streets for business; probably it lacked markets; and it was without great secular public works. It was rather a great agglomeration of shrines and other buildings for religious exercises. The permanent residents were probably priests and other functionaries discharging religious and magical offices. The ordinary people lived in small rural settlements separated at considerable distances from one another in the forest or "bush." These people came into the shrine-cities to watch or perhaps to take some part in the rituals conducted by the priests.

Thus we first see, although but dimly, the Yucatec Maya when out of their original precivilized folk condition there had developed a native civilization, the beginnings of an urban dimension of living. Yet, although we cannot see the earlier period directly, we may distinguish, as historically necessary, the period of the precivilized folk society from the period of the theocratic aboriginal state.

Is it possible to say something about the moral system, including perhaps the religion, of the earlier period? Its very broad outlines may be described. The principal source is the isolated Maya, who today exhibit many elements of

belief and practice that cannot have been introduced by
Europeans and that are confirmed as aboriginal by what
is said about these Maya by the first Spanish witnesses of
their way of life at the time of the Conquest. For the very
reason that the Maya continued to live in bush villages
before their own cities rose and after those cities fell, before and after the Spanish conqueror and Christian missionary had come, customs and beliefs that were intimately
connected with the life of the agricultural villager persisted, in general character, throughout all the period of
Maya history here under review. The names of the rain
gods, the beings that protected cornfield and village, the
cosmogonic conceptions, the cycle of agricultural rituals,
certain conceptions of disease and purification—such elements of belief and practice are reported by Bishop Landa
and others in the sixteenth century; and these we find again
in villages studied in the twentieth century.[9] It is the religion that I am here attempting to describe, the religion
as a sort of guide or evidence as to the intensity, localism,
and degree of integration of the whole moral order. As to
the values more generally, I can say almost nothing as to
the changes over these two thousand or more years. I think
that in certain respects these moral conceptions changed
in important ways when the Maya became Mexican peasants. But there may have been earlier transformations
of the ethical life concerning which nothing is now
known.

Apparently the students of the Roman religion at the
time when Rome was only a little settlement on the hills
above the Tiber have also inferred the religion of that folk
period from fragmentary inscriptions and especially from
what appear as survivals in the religion of the later periods.
So, to suggest the possibilities of comparative generaliza-

tion, I will attempt to characterize the Maya and the Roman in a single set of words.

In the precivilized folk society, European and American, the community was the village, and within the village the moral order was self-consistent and strong. In the absence of a specialized group of literate priests, all members of the community shared the same essential beliefs, and the practice of religion was open to all. Nature had its sacred and personal attributes; almost any aspect of nature was thought to have its indwelling, awe-compelling force. The Maya saw the bush and the village as under the protection of more personalized supernatural beings (*balamob*); the sky was upheld at the four corners of the physical universe by other beings (*pahuatunob*), and the rain was poured upon the earth by the rain gods (*chaacob*), beings who might grant or withhold material well being and who were therefore to be especially appealed to and propitiated. Lesser supernatural beings were associated with the deer that were hunted, with certain sacred trees (the ceiba), serpents and certain birds, frogs, and tortoises—these last being associated with water and the fertility that water brings. So the ancient Roman saw forces—numina—in groves, streams, trees, and certain sacred animals. The specialized Roman deities at this period were connected with the earth and the heavens, or with agriculture (Jupiter was a sky god, Mars, an agricultural deity); and the same may be said of the named deities of the ancient Maya. At the Roman hearth, the cupboard, and the door, there stood other protective beings; the penates suggest the protective *balamob* of the Maya; the lares suggest the Maya protectors of the crossways and of the forest clearings. The relationship between gods and men was conceived as the maintenance of a harmony through offerings and prayers;

the pious Maya today uses the word *taman* for this state of harmony; the Romans spoke of the *pax deum,* and of the piaculum, the offering which evidenced the sacred contract such as is described for the ancient Romans and such as also the Mayan villager now reaffirms, and probably anciently constantly reaffirmed, between the deities who grant rain and health and harvest, and himself. Sickness was, in both Roman and Mayan village, in part regarded as a consequence of moral transgression, and cure was accordingly purification: *lustratio* was the Roman rite; the Maya have and had their ancient *loh* ceremony—a rite whereby evil influence is cleansed from the sick man or the afflicted household or settlement. Ceremonies were domestic, or celebrated by the people of the settlement for the whole settlement. The offerings of the paterfamilias to the *genius* of the family or to the numina of door or hearth are not matched by what I know of the Maya, but the domestic first-fruit offerings, which the Maya still make, suggest a Roman domestic religious ceremony which may have been more important in ancient times. In both villages the agricultural annual round gave the occasions for ceremonies to ensure good crops; at this early period the Roman Ambarvalia was a purificatory rite to assure productivity of fields and animals, and the Saturnalia was a fertility rite. So, too, the Maya made offerings when the bush was burned before planting, when the maize was planted, when the young corn sprouted, and when the harvest was assured. As the primitive calendar of months, based on the solar year, with agricultural importance, had by this time come into use among the Roman villagers, so the agricultural calendar of eighteen periods of twenty days plus one period of five days was followed by the precivilized Maya. It is probable that in Yucatan the divinatory compound series of thirteen numbers and twenty names had also come into being, probably independently of the study of the solar year, and this the villagers used to guide them in choosing days fortunate or unfortunate for this venture or for that. The two kinds of knowledge represented by these two elements of calendar, the solar year of eighteen-day months, and the divinatory cycle of 260 double symbols of good or ill, were probably separately maintained by two separate kinds of developing specialists. The combination of the two calendrical conceptions into one system and the extraordinary, complex development of this compound system in esoteric calendar and astronomy were the work of literati of the next, or first urban, period.

These, then, in a few casual words confusing Maya and Roman in a manner to outrage any good historian, are the outlines of the religion and perhaps seen through the religion, of some parts of the moral order, of the precivilized folk society in two parts of the world. It is a state of society in which the technical order is still subordinated to the moral order, in which the local community is a single, well-integrated moral community, without separation of classes by important differences in knowledge or in faith, in which skepticism and sense of necessity to defend or to modify the ethical ideas are presumably absent. Yet while the people are religious, the religious rituals in these two cases are practical in that they are concerned with health and wealth.

For the Maya, the second period to be distinguished is the period now called the Classical. It began about 320 A.D. when, so far as we know, first appear initial series dates in the early shrine cities. With regard to the interest the period has for us here, we may say it did not end until the coming of the Spaniards, but certain changes took place in the three or four centuries before that event which will concern us. I speak now of the whole urban period. Out of the folk society has developed an indigenous civilization. The villagers continue to carry on their rituals in their villages and in their maize fields, and many of the deities they address are those named in the much more complex rites carried out in the shrine cities. The city priest and the rural farmer see the same quadrilateral, layered universe, appeal to the same rain-gods, regard anxiously the same cycle of the seasons, and conceive the duty of man to be the maintenance by ritual of the sacred contract between the gods and man. But now the priest in the shrine city has the authority to manage the principal ceremonies, on behalf of the whole community, rural dwellers included. The religion has now a public and tribal function. Some part of the whole religious and moral life is maintained for the common people, by specialists who do not live among them. Moreover, these specialists are now writers, and calculators, and thinkers. They have taken the elements of the solar year and the invention of the 260-day cycle, have combined these, and have measured off the time of tradition and the time of mythical prophecy. Under their direction the initial series dates are now written. Some of these inscriptions contain what we might call typographical errors—characters in wrong positions, or substitutions. These garblings of the inscriptions may have been deliberately made for magical or religious reasons, or they may merely suggest the gap in knowledge that was coming about between the priest and the workman who carved the glyph. At any rate, there has now developed a series of intellectual and religious conceptions about the movements of the heavenly bodies and the interrelations of time periods themselves of staggering complexity. The mental world of the literati and that of the rural farmer have now separated. The ethics and world view of the two are still at bottom the same, but the complex conceptions of the literati now reach far beyond anything of which the rustic could conceive.

This is the period in which the moral order becomes managed by an elite, or functional class, and in which the reflection and systematization accomplished by the literati have added a new dimension to the ethical and intellectual life. The moral order has now a public phase connected with deliberate policy. Spinden [10] thinks he has the evidence for a congress of astronomer-priests at Copan in the early centuries of the Christian era, when certain local differences as among Maya cities in the writing of certain calendrical corrections were ironed out and there was adopted a general plan to be followed by all communities represented in the conference. It is the presence of two things—the state and speculative thought—and of two new types of men—the statesman and the philosopher—that distinguishes this period, this later institutionalization of moral order. I would venture to compare this period in Yucatan with the period of the Roman city-state. The old *genius* of the family is now matched by a *genius populi romani;* the cult of the hearth has its public phase in the vestal virgins; Jupiter becomes a god of war and victory, and the warlike aspect of Mars turns uppermost. Public rituals are performed by magistrates to a people now more passive in participation. Religion is now, in short, a way of making citizens. The moral order is under public management. Literacy has produced speculative thinkers, and skepticism is not uncommon.

Because Rome was less isolated than the ancient Maya cities, there had begun in this period of the state and the speculative thinker, an introduction into Rome of those elements of foreign religion which, at the corresponding period in Yucatan, we cannot see from the archaeological record. When the city-state develops, Roman religion is already a mixture, including many Etruscan elements. So the two periods are not quite equivalent. There began earlier at Rome than in the Maya area that intrusion of elements alien to the indigenous culture by which I would distinguish the third Maya period, the period including and following the entrance into the Yucatan peninsula of Nahua culture and religion from Mexico to the west. I will call it the period of syncretism. Expanding civilizations have come into contact with one another, and elements of belief and practice have been learned by the people of one civilization from those of another. But they have entered without that violence, deracination, or sweeping missionary effort which breaks down a moral order almost entirely. The foreign elements have been introduced slowly enough, or locally enough, so that within not many generations they have been incorporated into the tradition generally prevailing in the community. In Yucatan we see the new cult of Mexican origin in the architectual adornments of later buildings at Chichen Itza and at other sites in northern Yucatan. The sense of invasion, of being led into new rites and beliefs, must have been strong in the tenth or eleventh century when first these conquering invaders made their appearance. But by the time of the coming of the Spaniards, the new cult had been incorporated into the moral order. Yet hints of a continuing sense of a conflict in the tradition appear to us. There was a secret interrogatory of candidates for high office to establish, through their knowledge of Nahua words brought in by the invaders, their claim to office. A fertility cult of the invaders had esoteric and erotic connotations to the Maya of the older local tradition. But on the whole there was again, in the year 1500, one culture in the peninsula, a unified moral order.

This third period, of syncretism, makes me think of the Roman religion during the period of the expansion of Rome to the end of the Second Punic War. Bailey recognizes this as a definable period. Commerce and contact with peoples outside the peninsula had brought about the incorporation into Roman religion of Greek cults—of Demeter, Dionysus, Persephone, and the cult of the sibylline books. New rituals were introduced: one in which images of gods were exhibited on couches and presented with food; and the *supplicatio*, in which the people asked divine aid at the temples. There was an adjustment of the alien gods to older Roman identifications of deity. There was a multiplication of the idioms of ritual. But essentially the religion, and the moral order related to religion, remained compelling and more or less unified.

This much of the development of the moral order—the naive moral order of the folk followed by the addition of a public and state-managed moral order with speculative intellectual developments, accompanied or followed by more or less syncretism of foreign elements with native elements—is probably characteristic of the rise of any indigenous civilization. It is civilization in the early phase while yet the process by which moral order is built up and integrated prevails over disintegrating influences. Perhaps something like it took place earlier in Egypt and in Mesopotamia. In primary and in secondary centers of civilization the moral order of the folk puts forth its civilization, however it may be stimulated from older centers, and as the town and city appear, so appear the state cult, the managed religion, the speculative development of ideas rooted in the folkways, and the incorporation of more and more foreign elements into a system of ideas still integrated and locally characteristic.

A new stage is marked when the disintegrating influences overcome those making for integration, with resulting relative decline in the moral order. It is the period in which Toynbee's proletariats, internal and external, become numerous. New ethical and religious systems have been imported in such variety that faiths compete with one another, and no system covers all the round of life for the whole community. There are now some people who believe some part of one system, or some part of another, or believe in none. Ancient traditional forms are repeated with their meanings lost. The more educated become rational or skeptical. In Rome this condition prevailed from the Second Punic War to the end of the Republic. The disasters of the Second Punic War were a blow to the social order and shook the moral order. Omens and portents multiplied, indicating the unrest and loss of moral certainty. Elements of the old religion struggled with the orgiastic cults, the mystery religions, for acceptance. The old calendrical cult that had arisen in the folkways of the ancient village-dwelling Romans appeared now in popular celebrations of city people, but the connection with the ancient agricultural life was lost. Plutarch speculated as to what might have been the meaning of the Lupercalia. It appeared to him much as Halloween appears to us. Cicero considered whether augury had any validity and defended religion as necessary to maintain society. The official religion was conducted by politicians; the priesthoods were offices of secular power. Many educated people withdrew from all this. Stoicism was a reflective philosophy for the conduct of life under conditions of moral decay. Something called "the religion of the poets" appeared, a self-conscious pseudo religion.

Such a period of break-up of the moral order we cannot describe for the Maya of Yucatan. What corresponds to it, the period immediately after the Spanish Conquest, was occasioned by a sudden, violent, and disruptive invasion of a people from a civilization very different from that which was native. It would be hard to compare it with events in Imperial Rome even if we had the facts about it. And we do not have the facts. The conversion of the Indians to Catholicism is presented to us chiefly in self-justificatory accounts written by the conqueror or the converter. Some of the conversions were not as far-reaching in their effects on the converted as the missionaries liked to believe, and in the more remote villages life was not greatly disturbed. Yet for the natives as a whole, the destruction of the images of their gods, the prohibition of ritual dances, the forced communities under Spanish mission rule, the labor on haciendas, and especially the almost complete removal of their priestly and philosophic elite—what A. V. Kidder has called the decapitation of Maya society—must have constituted a drastic revolution of life. In certain of the books of Chilam Balam written down after the Conquest we read the words in which the native laments the breakdown of his old moral order:

Then everything was good. Then they adhered to the dictates of their reason. There was no sin; in the holy faith their lives were passed. There was then no sickness; they had then no aching bones. . . . At that time the course of humanity was orderly. The foreigners made it otherwise when they arrived here. They brought shameful things when they came.[11]

Then with the true God, the true *Dios,* came the beginning of our misery.[12]

And the Indian narrator proceeds to list the miseries which began with the European invasion, from purse-snatching to forced debts, compulsory service, and carnal sin. In Yucatan after the Conquest, culture—now a mixed culture—came again to be built up. During the next three centuries integration prevailed over disintegration: a more or less unified way of life came to prevail again in the peninsula. The technical order continued to grow, but its growth, by slow development of political forms, slow economic progress, and slow introduction of new material tools, was not such as to overcome the tendency of the moral order to heal itself. Yucatan in colonial times was a backwater in the currents of advancing industrial civilization. Urbanization continued, but both in the city and in the country there developed relatively consistent ways of life. The sharply distinguished social classes of the city pursued distinct and yet fundamentally united ethical paths. In the villages Catholic Christianity was accommodated to the indigenous religion and world view. The Indians, now peasants in relationship to the more Hispanic city, reached the emphasis of those values characteristic of the peasant which I mentioned earlier. In the villages most remote from the city, where the later influences of urbanization hardly reached, the unification of elements of living derived in part from Spain and in part from indigenous tradition became nearly complete. Spanish prayer, Christian cross, and ceremonies to the pagan gods of rain and cornfield came to form parts, inseparable in the thinking of the villager, of a single way of life, expressions of one compelling moral order. These remote villages were remade folk societies, folk societies in the same sense and in similar degree to those folk societies of entirely indigenous tradition which stood there during the Maya Old

Empire, long before the coming of Columbus. In the most remote of such villages the moral order represented once more that type of moral order represented also in the precivilized Roman settlement. Yet, while this reintegration of culture, this restitution of moral order, was going on, at the same time the later urban influences were affecting all communities in Yucatan, and of course most strongly the towns and the provincial city. The twentieth century saw great changes in Merida, the one large city. The traditional ways of life underwent such disorganization that here it becomes possible to say again that the disintegrating tendencies overcame the tendencies toward cultural and moral integration. I cannot here take the time to develop this assertion except to say that, once more considering religion as an index to the state of the moral order, Merida suggests to me the Rome of late Imperial times. Catholicism remained a genuine religion for some, a convenient convention, a mere form, for others, and the Catholic religion came to be a sort of party, competing with evangelical Protestantism, revolutionary materialism, and other faiths for the allegiance of the people. In the lively interest in spiritualism, theosophy, and other new cults which was to be observed in Merida, and in the developing skepticism and general disbelief, I see again a parallel with later Rome.

The account I have just sketched of the history of Yucatan—now setting aside any comparisons with conditions in Rome—may be summarized as follows. The folk society, with moral order strong and dominant over technical order, gave rise, within itself, to a civilization, the moral order accordingly developing an aspect of public management by an elite, or class, who carried forward a specialized speculative expansion of some of the ideas of native tradition. Throughout pre-Columbian times the technical order developed very slowly and elements of culture introduced from alien traditions were incorporated into the indigenous culture, leaving the moral order substantially unshaken. From the catastrophic disintegration accomplished by the Conquest, the moral order slowly recovered in the relative isolation of Yucatan during three hundred years. But meanwhile the effects of the urbanization of modern Western civilization began, and continued, with accelerating effect, to threaten the re-fashioned moral order. Some of the consequences of these new influences were the subject of the study of four communities in Yucatan, the results of which have been published.[13]

The changing fortunes of the moral order in Yucatan have been here presented as affected by two things which have not been separated: the expanding technical order; and the multiplication of contacts and communications. It is perhaps not possible to separate them, or at least not necessary to separate them. As commerce grows, as means of communication and transportation are multiplied and improved, as political authority is extended over wider areas, people are always moved around and brought into new communication with one another.

But this is not the point about this summary of the history of culture and the moral order in Yucatan which seems to me worth challenging. There seems to me in the generalized account of the relationships between technics and ethics into which I have ventured, a serious error or deficiency. Before I try to state this deficiency, I will summarize the position so far taken, now not in terms of Yucatan, but in terms of the effect of civilization on the moral order everywhere. According to this conception, the integrity and the compelling force of the moral order in society are functions of isolation and a slow rate of development of the technical order. According to this conception, the moral order flourishes as the society is shut away from outside influences and as the technical order develops not at all or only slowly. In contrast, either when new ideas are rapidly introduced and people of different traditions are moved around into pervasive new communications with one another, or else when the technical order develops rapidly within an indigenous civilization, the moral order is thrown into confusion and its authority declines. Of course these two kinds of happenings tend to occur together. The former—the sudden intrusion of the invader who makes over a conquered society—was the important fact in the disorganization of native moral order which must have occurred when the Spaniards conquered Yucatan. It was the fact that caused the Melanesians reported by Rivers to lose interest in life. The second happening, the rapid development of the technical order of an indigenous civilization, combined with the intrusion of alien ideas in the case of the decline of the moral order of Imperial Rome.

This simple view of what goes on generally amounts to saying, in short, that the ethical convictions of man strengthen or weaken solely with the events of technological development and with increased or decreased communications. This view identified civilization solely with the technical order. It makes civilization an invariable enemy of the moral order. It sees the results of civilization as a decline in moral order only.

This view seems to me correct insofar at least as it sees that in human history as between the technical order and the moral order it is the technical order that takes a certain lead. We do see that there has been a largely accumulative and accelerated development of the technical order. We do see that changes in the moral order have been brought about thereby. The moral order, if one speaks figuratively, seems to be striving to keep up with the technical order. And this in turn stimulates new developments in the technical order. Trade and travel bring people into relationships with each other with resulting disruption of the local religious and ethical life, and then some political invention—foreign rule, or an imperial system, perhaps—is developed, itself a feature of the technical order, to take account of these new and probably troubling relationships, moral as well as technical, among men. Under the concept of the "cultural lag" we study some of these dislocations and readjustments. It is ordinarily the technical order that gets ahead so as to produce the lag.

Moreover, it seems likely—it being such a commonplace of observation—that that part of the technical order which is expressed in political institutions tends to come temporarily to a halt at some point in development where the moral order can more or less catch up with it. The unit of political life tends to become identified with a people who share a common moral life, including the sense that they share one. So the tribe, the city-state, the nation are such approximate identifications of equivalent units of society, peoples that are both a technical and a moral unit. Yet as one looks at any one of these politico-moral societal types as it appears to predominate at some place or time, one sees that the technical order, in the form of exchange of goods and in the conflict of war, has already gone beyond the politico-moral unit, which is already inadequate to keep people from enjoying the fruits of the exchange or even the security of peace; and one begins to look forward to the extension of the moral order to larger societal units, which will in turn call for political inventions. Today some people, recognizing that the technical order has gone far beyond the national state, and that its destructive power threatens everyone, begin to argue that the peace of the world must be planned by all the people of the world. As did Wendell Willkie, some of us begin to talk as if there were a world community, a global *Gesellschaft.* And then, looking at the fact that these visions have come and begin to be transmuted into plans for action, one is required to admit that the fact that people speak as if world order and world peace must and will come about is itself influential in history, a fact in the interaction of technical and moral order. The idea that a world community is necessary is an idea created by developments in the technical order. This idea in turn influences the actual moral order to develop in its direction, and helps to bring about political inventions, United Nations, or possible charters of a universal federal government that would both express and create the enlarging moral order. We have encountered the conception of ideas as forces in history.

It is the role of ideas in history which demands consideration in revising the more materialist interpretation of the broad outlines of human history which I have just been attempting to sketch. In this sketch the moral order has been presented as the helpless victim or the passive creature of changes in the technical order. To what extent must we correct this sketch by introducing the conception that ideas, generated early in the course of technological development, became themselves causative agents of further transformations in human living?

This immense and long-considered problem may be here separated into two parts: as the question is asked of human history before the urban revolution; and as it is asked of human history following the urban revolution. Childe, the leading student of the prehistoric period, recognizes that in a society its "economy affects, and is affected by, its ideology." [14] But he thinks of the ideology as chiefly more or less adaptive to the technical (economic) order. At most the ideology, the idea in history, may impede changes in the technical order. This view seems to me inadequate, but it is certainly more plausible for the precivilized period. At any rate, we have no way to see seminal ideas shape the history of the cave men. If we are to form any basis for inferences as to the force of ideas in history before the urban revolution, the inference can be based only on what is suggested to us by the little we know of ideas in the history of isolated surviving primitive peoples. Some examination of this aspect of the problem will be offered in the fifth chapter.

For the recent part of human history, not just after but long after the urban revolution, the role of ideas in history is obvious to hundreds of scholars. It is a great theme of Western historiography and philosophic writing. For the West, at least, and certainly after Ionia and Athens, a purely materialist view of history is untenable. Whitehead has traced the history and impact of certain of the great ideas of the West. "The distinguishing mark of modern civilization is the number of institutions whose origin can be traced to the initial entertainment of some idea." [15] With the development of writing, literate and reflective people, and enlarged opportunities to travel, to communicate, and to think things over, the power of ideas to create ideas and of ideas to create institutions, greatly increased. Some of these ideas—some of the powerful ones—have to do with the right, the good, and the true. We may describe this change by saying that from now on the moral order is self-regenerative. While the technical order continues to expand, and to have profound influence on the moral communities of mankind, these communities now have a new power to create values that in turn demand, whether they be successful or no, the control and limitation of the development of the technical order.

Here I assume only the very modest task of emphasizing some of the ways in which, after the rise of cities, ideas are influential in history. The needed correction of the sketch already given as to the characteristic relations between technical order and moral order is this: It is not enough to say that the technical order is destroyer of the moral order. It is not enough to identify civilization with development in the technical order alone. It is also to be recognized that the effects of the technical order include the creation of new moral orders. Through civilization people are not only confused, or thrown into disbelief and a loss of will to live. Through civilization also people are stimulated to moral creativeness. Civilization is also ideas in history. It is new vision, fresh and bold insights, perceptions and teachings of religious and ethical truth which could not have come about had there not been the expansion of the technical order which is the first and obvious aspect of civilization. To write these things is to write things so obvious that I am almost ashamed to write them. They need to be asserted, however, if we are to connect, in some degree, the views of human history seen by archaeologist, historian, and ethnologist.

When began the influence of creative ideas in the rise of the first civilizations? When, in the history of mankind, does it become impossible to see the development of civilization simply as a sort of automatic and inevitable growth of the technical order? Archaeology shows us the ever-widening area within which the prehistoric and ancient peoples exchanged goods, and it shows the increase in the quantity and variety of these goods. It shows us the improvement in the tools of production, in the construction of public works, in the rapidly increasing migrations and inter-communications of peoples of different heritages. With written documents to aid, we are shown the extensions of political authority, the first kingdoms and empires. But when do ideas enter history? For one thing, we may ask when and where in the ancient world did a collective sense of economic rivalry first appear? When it appeared, there was an idea in history. Then, to the multitude of separately and personally motivated exchanges of goods and services was added a competitive spirit characteristic of a people, a trait of culture, an idea of a whole people that it was its purpose and perhaps its destiny to extend its commercial and perhaps other influence over other peoples. And when did such a conception become connected with a policy and a program of political expansion? John Wilson, discussing a change in the state of mind of the ancient Egyptians after the Hyksos conquest, writes of a "psychosis for security" which developed among the Egyptians and that found, under the Empire, a later expression in a sense "of a 'manifest destiny' to extend one culture in domination over another." The god-king and the other gods "supported the extension of the frontiers of the land." [16] A sense of manifest destiny is an idea in history. In reading ancient history during Hellenic and Roman times do we not encounter it?

A consciousness in a people that it is their mission to extend their rule, their customs, their kind of law and justice, over peoples different from themselves is such an idea as now supplements and guides the automatic extensions of the technical order. It controls and it justifies an expansion engined by power—commercial, military, political. Surely, as in the extension of Hellenic culture into Asia through Alexander, or in the expansion of Western civilization with the aid of such ideas as the white man's burden or the manifest destiny of the United States, it has great consequences for the moral order, and it may, as in the conception of Roman law, have an ethical component within itself. But these ideas are not primarily ideas of religious and ethical creativeness; they are ideas after the technical fact. And all of them contain an assumption as to the superiority of right or privilege of the expanding people over others. And one ventures to say that all of them fail in the long run.

I suppose that we do find ideas of true ethical and religious creativeness within ancient civilized societies. Where an individual with that great concentration of power which is not possible in a precivilized society has an idea with regard to the moral order, creative or destructive, he may attempt a revolution in the moral order. The two examples that commonly come to mind of such revolutions attempted by ancient rulers—the monotheistic reforms of Akhnaton, and the attempt of the Ch'in Emperor, Shih Huang Ti, to bring Confucian teaching to an end in China —ended in failure. Is it not true that the individually led creativity in the moral order, which lasts, comes, not from the people who are in the center of the expanding civilization and who have the power, but from people who feel themselves outside it? Confucian teaching, as declared in that doctrine called *tao-t'ung*, "orthodox transmission of the way," was formulated by a scholar-gentry who had lost, or had never had, political power. To become effective as a teacher, Gautama Buddha had to give up material power.

There is a certain marginal or even proletarian character in Toynbee's terms about the world religions. And each of them taught the inclusion of all mankind in the new moral order. These religions and new ethical teachings arose in a millennium when trade, travel, and conquest had broken down local cultures, when thousands of people had lost the sense of purpose in life. They may be recognized as the first great expansions of moral order to transcend the local community and the local culture and to embrace all humanity. And the immense creativeness they represent was made possible by the expansive and disintegrative nature of civilization itself.

The anthropologist encounters this creativity of the disintegrated folk society in the form of nativistic movements. The impact of civilization upon the primitive societies results in part in the stimulation of new ideas, new religions, and ethical conceptions. Not all primitive peoples helplessly accept the conqueror's ways, or passively die out, or go down fighting with the spear or the gun. These are common endings of their stories, but there are many cases of moral regeneration, of fresh religious leadership. In 1819 the Paiute prophet Wodziwob preached the coming end of the world, the destruction of the white man, and the return of the Indian dead. The new believers were to be protected by performing certain rituals. This general doctrine was restated in 1890 by a new prophet, and the Ghost Dance cult then spread to many Indian peoples, all suffering from the disintegration of their old life and the loss of the sense of life's purpose. Similarly, a little later in New Guinea prophets arose among disorganized natives to preach the end of the white man, the return of the native dead, and a way to security and a new future through the performance of certain rituals.

These movements are sometimes seen as wish fulfill-ments, as projections of a hope of escape from frustration and despair. So, no doubt, they are. The doctrine is always a representation of what despairing people want to happen. But also these movements are to be seen as instances of moral creativeness. They represent, in limited and local cases, the power of human intelligence and insight to pro-vide a fresh vision of a moral order. Toynbee, to whom these prophetic Indians are among the external proletariats of the Western world, so sees them. He is impressed with the disposition of the leaders of these native movements to preach peace and renunciation of the material powers of the white man.

Civilization is creator to the moral order as well as de-stroyer. The breakdown of old local cultures is also an en-largement of man's view of the world. Indian tribes that before knew each other only as enemies came, through civilization, to know each other as fellow sufferers. And among the deracinated and the dispossessed, the internal proletariats of early civilizations, came to be forged, out of what civilization did to them, a new sense of common cause. The very pain of deprivation is the birth pang of a new thought, a fresh teaching. The new teaching tends to be more inclusive than was any of the old moral orders of any one primitive society. In the Ghost Dance, in the Peyote Cult, American Indians of different traditions and lan-guages find a new brotherhood, though still qualified and much limited in scope. The new sense of common cause may take a political form and become a secular nationalistic movement. Then its inclusiveness will be limited by the boundaries of that group which seeks freedom from domi-nation or admission to the community of nations. But the teaching of the fresh insight may be and remain religious.

81

Then, but not always, it may include not just these people but all people. On the one hand the creative movement may center its hope on the tribal messiah, on the miraculous overturn of the oppressor's power, on the freedom of the local community. Then it will only restore a limited moral order. Or, on the other hand, it has happened in a few cases that the ethical content of the new idea, remaining apart from a program to achieve a political objective, has become strengthened and universalized. God became universal among the oppressed Jews, and out of the immense creative idea of a single universal deity and a universal moral imperative arose Christianity.

One ventures to say that from the record of history it appears that those ideas in history which have the most force are those which speak for everyone. The concept of manifest destiny is an idea that will unite the forces of a self-chosen people, whether Egyptians or Americans, but it will do so only toward ends which are self-limiting, for such a limited idea will in the end arouse the human aspirations of the excluded and the oppressed. On its frontiers, both those within and those without, move against it the creative powers of the human mind. The very universality that appeals to those who have nothing to lose but their chains results in a fresh affirmation of that other kind of idea in history which has a long life and a great influence.

Such are the ideas in history of which Whitehead writes. He tells us of the career in history of the conception of the dignity of human nature. He makes us see that such an idea has power of development that is recognizable in and yet apart from the particular occasions on which it is enunciated. Once in history, such ideas are always there, "at once gadflies irritating, and beacons luring, the victims among whom they dwell." [17] It is the idea itself which is the long-lived actor on the human stage. In this way, says White-head, the idea of human dignity abolishes slavery and goes on to demand that there be no more second-class citizens, that forced labor of the innocent cease, and that the in-dignity of racial segregation come to an end.

So, following Whitehead's lead, we may suspect that other ideas of corresponding power and endurance are already at work among us: the idea of permanent peace, also the idea of universal human responsibility, to balance and extend the creative idea of universal human rights. The existence of these ideas does not allow us to predict that they will one day be realized in fact, for, to some of us at least, man's freedom includes the possibility and the power to destroy himself, and the possibility and the power to continue somehow to muddle along. When some men utter these ideas, others speak of them as bold and forward-directing dreams are always spoken of: they are unrealistic, fanciful, Utopian. So they are; but also they are among the movers and shakers of human affairs. And their strength lies in their universality.

These great ideas in history are possible only in civiliza-tion. The precivilized and the isolated preliterate are unaf-fected by them. The urban revolution resulted in a great transformation whereby the minds of men in local com-munities came to be shaped by reformist ecumenical ideas expressed in written word and preached in far-flung teach-ings. Only civilization could bring about the circumstances of moral conflict in which these ideas could arise and the means for their transmission and reflective development. Civilization is a new dimension of human experience. The great idea, moving among many traditions and in newly troubled minds, is now an agent of change, a shaper of the moral order.

I V

Primitive World View
and Civilization

WHEN we speak of "world view" we make one kind of attempt to characterize a traditional way of life. "World view" is one of those terms which are useful in asserting something of what is most general and persistent about a people. Such terms are related to the "culture" of which the anthropologist makes so much in that each represents the effort to describe that way of life, as it differs from other ways of life, generally and taken as a whole. If we try to say something about the important qualities of a people, we have not many choices as to the manner in which to say it. We can attempt to say something that includes all aspects of that mode of life; we can mention all the principal customs and institutions of that society. Then we find ourselves describing at length "the culture," as anthropologists have often done. Or we can seek out some few dominating or underlying parts of these customs and institutions, some of the more general and persisting conceptions, and the appearance of these in practices and institutions. Then we find ourselves talking about fundamental themes or patterns. Or we can place emphasis on the normative aspect of this great whole, and then "ethos" appears, the system of values. And, in the writings of still others are to be found attempts to define the manner and forms of thought characteristic of a people. Professor Northrop has attempted to distinguish Orient from Occident in terms of a difference in basic conceptions of the nature of things.[1] In this connection we may also recall the many contrasts in thinking asserted to exist between primitive or ancient peoples on the one hand and modern civilized peoples on the other, including those put forward by Franz Boas, L. Levy-Bruhl, Hans Kelsen and Henri Frankfort, and also the recent studies by Benjamin Whorf [2] and many others of linguistic patterns and their connections with national or ethnic modes of thought. And, finally in this short list, I mention the interest recently directed toward the characterization of a people, of a way of life, as if we were characterizing a single human being. The attempt to describe "national character" is of this sort. In that case a people is represented in terms of one generalized personality. The words that are then appropriate are the words with which we describe some one of our friends or acquaintances. In that branch of the enquiry, the description is sometimes explicitly made in terms of a "personality type," and the explanation of the formation of the type is found, perhaps, in the mode of rearing children.[3]

The culture of a people is, then, its total equipment of ideas and institutions and conventionalized activities. The ethos of a people is its organized conceptions of the Ought. The national character of a people, or its personality type, is the kind of human being which, generally speaking, occurs in that society. The "world view" of a people, yet another of this group of conceptions, is the way a people characteristically look outward upon the universe. If "culture" suggests the way a people look to an anthropologist, "world view" suggests how everything looks to a people, "the designation of the existent as a whole." [4] It is true that the term has been so broadly used as to include a good deal of what is more particularly emphasized by one or another of the other terms I have just mentioned; included in "world view" may be the conceptions of what ought to be as well as of what is; and included may be the characteristic ways in which experiences are kept together or apart—the patterns of thought—and the affective as well as the cognitive aspect of these things also.[5] "World view" may be used to include the forms of thought and the most comprehensive attitudes toward life. A world view can hardly be conceived without some dimension in time, some idea of past and of future; and the phrase is large enough and loose enough to evoke also the emotional "set" of a people, their disposition to be active, or contemplative, or resigned, to feel themselves distinct from what is "out there," or to identify themselves closely with the rest of the cosmos.

But if there is an emphasized meaning in the phrase "world view," I think it is in the suggestion it carries of the structure of things as man is aware of them. It is in the way we see ourselves in relation to all else. Every world view is a stage set. On that stage myself is an important character; in every world view there is an "I" from which the view is taken. On the stage are other people, toward whom the view is directed. And man, as a collective character, is upon the stage; he may speak his lines very loudly, or he may be seen as having but a minor part among other parts. On the stage also are things seen as not the same as man, though they may be seen more or less like him. To speak yet more concretely about the nature of world view is to use words and conceptions which may be appropriate to the world view that you and I know, and not to all world views; but this is a familiar kind of difficulty in the face of which we must proceed. In our own world view nature is pretty clearly seen as something different from man and as something toward which man takes a characteristic attitude. Unseen things are there too: beings, principles, trends, and destinies. History, with nature, is part of world view. All of this has a structure, an arrangement that the world view recognizes to persist and to have consequences for man. The thing about world view that is different from culture, ethos, or national character, is that it is an arrangement of things looked out upon, things in first instance conceived of as existing. It is the way the limits or "illimits," the things to be lived with, in, or on, are characteristically known. The difficulty of defining world view as something distinct from other aspects of the totality of group character is not the only difficulty in defining the conception. We are early confronted with the question: Whose world view are we talking about? For this is a characteristic as to which the individual men and women making up a society differ very much among themselves, and especially differ from one another in the more civilized societies. To let a list of customs and institutions stand for everybody in a society perhaps does not do too much injustice to individual differences, and the same may perhaps be said if we mention the paramount values of a people. To say "Liberty, Equality, and the Sovereignty of the People" may not be to say anything very precise, but these resounding nouns do probably stand for most Americans. The difficulty in characterizing a complex people in terms of a world view is something peculiar to that conception, namely, the fact that a world view becomes for the people who have it a matter of systematic and highly specialized reflective study and development. Would not a study of the historic beginnings of the systematization of ideas show that it is with cosmology rather than with ethical system or personality type that the beginning is made? There are people who work upon the world view and build it up into something different from what most of the people in that society see the cosmos to be. Whether this distinction between the reflective and the merely active is to be seen in different persons in even the most primitive societies, as Paul Radin has told us in his book on primitive man as philosopher,[6] or whether the difference between the speculative man and other people is less great in the nonliterate societies than he thinks, it is surely true that the difference is apparent to some degree among primitives and peasants and becomes very great in civilizations. I make a study of Maya Indians of Yucatan. One man of the village in particular is a thoughtful fellow; he really ruminates. When I ask him questions, his mind seems naturally to arrange things into systematic wholes. I find it easy to put down what he says, just because it is so well considered and makes such coherent sense. But does he really represent the other Indians who can say so much less to me about the world they inhabit? Ethnology is itself a building of world views into cosmologies. For we might at once accept the term that philosophers use and speak of a "cosmology" when we mean a rational attempt to deal with ultimate problems of nature—to make intellectual effort toward comprehension of the cosmos. Then there is already, in primitive society, at least some slight difference between the world view of most people and the cosmologies of the more thoughtful.

But, as civilization advances, the difference becomes greater. Shall we let the extraordinary cyclical and layered universe revealed to us as the thoughtful construct of the ancient Maya astronomer-mathematician stand for the world view of the Maya Indian villager and simple grower of maize? Shall we allow the *Summa* of St. Thomas and the *Divine Comedy* to represent the world view of the medieval European peasant? The account of the universe offered by modern physics, or the speculations of Descartes or of Kant to stand for the world view of modern Londoners or Detroit auto workers? Stated in this order, the three proposals are increasingly indefensible. In the case of modern man, the gap between the ordinary man's world view and the scientist's cosmology is very great indeed. But then, we know more, I should think, about the world view of the Navaho Indian than we know of the world view of the ordinary people of New York and Chicago. On the one hand I suppose we may assume that the developed cosmologies of physicist and philosopher have some influence, though indirect, on the way in which the uneducated and unreflective gaze out upon their universe. On the other, I suppose it might be easy to fall into the error of comparing the ethnologist's summation of the world view of the Navaho, which does more or less represent all Navaho, with the world view of Descartes or Percy Bridgman, which may represent in the one case chiefly Descartes and in the other a very few theoretical physicists. The anthropologist may be pardoned for fleeing for refuge among Indian or Andamanese, where what one man thinks is not too different from what most of them think. Yet he cannot avoid recognizing the importance, when he comes to speak of civilization, of the development of world views into cosmologies, and the intricate problems that appear when it is seen that in civilization specialized cosmologies affect the implicit world view or world views that are common in the society.

With this confession of difficulties, I turn now to the

89

question: What, if anything, is true of all world views? In choosing to put this question ahead of the many questions as to differences among world views, I think I conform to a trend. There is now in anthropology a disposition to consider questions of human universality. The interest in differences among people and how to account for them which has prevailed in the anthropology of this century seems now not quite enough. We begin once more to ask: What is true of all men? It is an old interest revived. That all societies are but variants of one another is a proposition that can be reconciled with one part of sound anthropological doctrine. The idea has been expressed in my discipline in attempts to find the universal culture pattern. At Yale University the records of a few hundred societies have been gone over to find what seems always to occur in human living; the rough analysis yielded at least seventy-five "elements common to all known cultures." [7] Other students of human differences turn to a consideration of the resemblances that one man bears to any other, and, after denying for quite a time that psychic unity exists, anthropologists now take a more sympathetic interest in something not too different, universal human nature. They even propose to find out which values are shared by all mankind, or at least are very general in human societies. And from yet another point of attack, human universality is reached. The emergency of the concept of basic personality type to describe the kind of personality which on the whole occurs in and reflects a given culture has led to the idea that all personalities, in all cultures, have some things in common. "The most basic of all personalities is the one connected with the fact that we are all human." [8] In this way also universal human nature is reached.

World view is one way to characterize universal human

nature. One of the aspects of human nature is to be found in the extent to which all men look out upon the same universe. If world view is universal, it should be possible to say what is true of all world views. There is not much to guide such an attempt. Concepts about world view are hardly developed, and comparative studies are barely begun. So any suggestions now put forward are almost random and are highly tentative. Nevertheless, something can be said about the common stage on which all mankind walks.

As suggested earlier, it seems necessary to suppose that every world view starts from the man who is the viewer and includes the idea of a self. Everybody looks out on a world from a viewpoint which he identifies with that being toward which, alone, he finds himself looking when he looks inward. This self is different from all else.[9] The analysis of the process by which that self is developed that G. H. Mead has given us includes no qualification to make it applicable only to people in G. H. Mead's social and cultural group. As we read what he writes, we at once suppose it to be true of people in every human society. And other elements in his analysis—the I and the Me, the generalized other—are also to be accepted as human universals. The world view includes also recognition of other people and a vision of people representing generalized roles. Should we now turn to a consideration of universal sentiments, such as C. H. Cooley liked to write about, we would be departing from world view to look at human nature as a kind of generalized personality. That I will not do here. Keeping to the conception of world view as a stage set, I go on to suppose that it always includes an arrangement of groupings of people according to qualitative differences connected with the groupings, not merely with the indi-

viduals who are grouped. Ways in which men may be characteristically seen as different from women in societies,
generally speaking, are suggested in one of Margaret
Mead's later books.[10] Other anthropologists, in emphasizing
the universality of that small and intimate kinship group
they call the nuclear family, suggest that the inevitable
stage setting includes whatever elements are common in
looking at the elder people, or the younger people, or the
siblings in that universal group. And it is probably safe to
say that among the groupings of people in every society are
always some that distinguish people who are my people,
or are more my people, from people who are not so much
my people. The We-They difference, in some form, arranges
the human elements on the universal stage.

One might next include in the universal world view a
recognition of difference between Man and Not-Man. I
cannot imagine a people that looks out upon a universe in
which no distinctions are made between men and animals
or invisible beings or the trees and the stars. The world
view always includes some conception of human nature.
The differences among world views in this respect are of
course quite as important as the resemblances. Indeed,
when one comes to consider great historical transformations in world view, it may be necessary to take note of
certain latter-day developments in man's view of the ways
in which he is different from other things.

Different as are the many ways in which men regard
themselves as partly in or largely out of something else
which we call Nature, and different as are the degrees and
kinds of interest in things around man, nevertheless it
seems safe to say that somehow it is the same world for
everybody. That earth and sky are two things, distinguishable; that water has its nature apart from earth; that fire

burns you if you touch it; that there is a horizon; that stars, sun, and moon make similar sorts of appearances with similar sorts of immediate consequences for men—however special and different are the things that may be said about these elements of world view in each particular people—all these are elements in the universals that are here being explored. So too one must think that every world view includes some spatial and temporal orientation; the cosmos has extension, duration, and periodicity. Further, as to the periodicity it is hard to suppose an entire absence of resemblance among world views, for the alternation of day and night, and that of the seasons, different as these things are in different places, are still alternations connected in the one case with the sun and in the other with cycles of time that do not vary within great limits.

It would be a one-sided sketch of Everyman's world view if it were left with no mention of the place of the universal human experiences in setting Everyman's stage. Birth and death are for everyone to confront, and, in lesser degree of universal impact, maturation and senescence, menstruation, menopause, and sexual intercourse. For those who do not experience these latter common experiences there is the experience of knowing that others do. But a recitation of what is part of our animal nature does not lead to what is the important human universal here. This lies in the degree and kind of resemblances among the attitudes taken toward these inevitable events. That birth is an occasion of hazard, that death is unavoidable and on the whole undesirable—these are mentions of the kinds of things that enter into this component of everybody's world view.

This summary of Everyman's world view has the vagueness of all universal characterizations of mankind that take some account of the great variations that exist. Yet it is something. It may be presented now in fewer words. It includes among other things recognition of the self and others; groupings of people, some intimate and near, others far and different; some usual ways of confronting the inevitable experiences of the human career; a confrontation of the Not-Man seen in some ordered relationships of component entities, this Not-Man including both some observed features such as earth, sky, day, night, and also invisible beings, wills, and powers.

Against such a vast shadow of generality the brilliance of each unique world view stands out. Each cries for emphasis of its special character. How different they are! Here are the Mountain Arapesh as described by Margaret Mead.[11] The world view of this Melanesian people takes little account of earth and sky, time or space, origins or explanations. They have no cosmology; they do little explaining as to how things came to be. Dr. Mead tells us that their outlook on the universe is primarily affective, not cognitive. She says that to them things are connected because the same emotional attitude is taken toward them. "Where a man's trees are, there his children will flourish." Next, this world view is concerned primarily, not with gods or physical universe, but with human nature, with human nature seen as dangerous and powerful sexuality which must be managed by both men and women in ritual and careful restraint so that procreation and prosperity may be assured. "Their whole attention has centered upon an internalized struggle between man and his human nature," aggressive and dangerous sexuality and parental and beneficent sexuality. Nevertheless, this world view, like others, includes special attitudes toward what we would call nature—in this case certain water holes or sharp declivities. And this world view includes, like others, beings neither men nor physical universe, here invisible beings that inhabit these places and, with the spirits of the kinship group, guard them. The Arapesh world view could be related to a triangle of man, nature, God, as I imagine all world views could be related. But this one centers upon man's nature, and the attitude is emotional; there is little intellectual systematization; the universe is very loosely structured.

If we set out to compare this world view with that of another primitive people not too different in mode of life, the Zuni, as their world view has been described by Ruth Bunzel [12] and others, we should see at once that the Zuni world view is more clearly structured, that man and nature are more equally included, and that in place of the management of sexuality the central place in the confrontation of the cosmos is occupied by the concept of preservation of the harmonious identification of God, nature, and man in one enduring recurrent system. And if we then brought forward the world view of the ancient Mesopotamians as described by Jacobsen, [13] we should again see the brilliance of a unique, coherent, and compelling cosmic conception, while we should see also the possibilities of comparison of Mesopotamian world view with world views of Arapesh and of Zuni. The ancient Mesopotamians conceived of the universe, says Jacobsen, as "an order of wills," as a great state. All things—salt, fire, sky, earth, man and also such notions as justice, righteousness, or the form of the circle—had will, character, and power. And all these things were arranged in a vast complex hierarchy of power. Again we have a world view in which man confronts a Not-Man including both natural objects and unseen beings and powers. Of course the system is far vaster, more systematic, than that of the Zuni. But with respect to amount of systematization and with respect to interest in that which is Not-Man, the Zuni world view stands apart from that of the Arapesh in the direction of the world view of the Mesopotamians. The confrontation is different in that, for the Zuni, what matters is performance of those rituals of the group which maintain harmonious identification of man, nature, and God. For the Mesopotamian, the emphasis was an obedience to power, earthly and celestial.

We advance our understanding of differences by seeking what is universal; and the attempt to find generalizing language in terms of which to compare things as to their resemblances as well as their differences leads us back again to a recognition of universals or part-universals. So with world view. As we begin to think about any two or three or four world views, against a background of even off-hand characterization of universal world view, we begin to find words to describe what is true of some world views but not true of others. Or—to put it more cautiously—we ask some questions which may prove helpful in advancing our understanding.

We might begin with the suggestion (that I have from Professor Daniel Boorstin) that we look first at this universal fact of confrontation: everywhere man looks out from himself on something else, and this looking out carries with it attitudes as to his relations with that on which he looks out. Then we might early ask two questions: (1) What does man confront? and (2) What is the relation he sees between himself and that which is confronted?

The first question receives content from comparison of the Arapesh with the Zuni. The Arapesh, we are told, primarily confront their own natures as bearers of power associated with sexuality. They are so concerned with confronting this that they let the rest of the cosmos slide, so to speak; sky, deity, distant powers, structures or destinies are not looked into. The Zuni look to God and nature as well as to man. Now this may be a distinction of some significance. The Chinese, we are told, have chosen human nature, or at least human relations, as the focus of world view, especially as the Confucian element is influential in their thinking, and, leaving aside the official cult, have not very much personalized nature into deity. The ancient civilizations of the West, on the other hand, confronted God and nature as much as or more than they confronted human nature. Yet in this regard there has come about in the West a great change. I think of the current emphasis on man's subjective states of mind and feeling, and of the concern today with personality as a central object of attention. Our world view comes to show a certain likeness to that of Margaret Mead's Arapesh, and in our own way we too have become concerned with the management of sexuality.

So far as such modern persons include the Not-Man in their world view, I imagine, without really knowing it to be true, that this other part of their world view, a conception of a physical universe, is off in a quite separate confrontation. Perhaps today people have not one world view but plural world views. Perhaps today among the literate of the West there are two stages for the drama of existence: a stage of stars, atoms, time, and space, through which man is whirled without obligation to him; and a stage of inner experience, unconnected with the other stage, where the problems and choices take place. On this latter stage other people are also characters taking part in the action, but possibly characters of declining importance.

The thing confronted may, I suppose, be seen and divided in many different ways. Important questions surely lie in the conceptions as to that part of the thing confronted which is distinguished from man. How is the Not-Man seen? Is it regarded as two distinguishable parts, Nature and God? Some Western thought has surely seen it so. Or is the Not-Man seen as a single system of entities both will and thing, both person and object, as apparently it is seen in many primitive and ancient societies? Or is the Not-Man wholly thing, without will or personal quality, as it becomes in the universe of modern secular minds?

The second question I have distinguished in considering the confrontation is as to the relation which man sees between himself and that which he confronts. There are no doubt many matters here. There is the relative emphasis on knowing and understanding what he confronts as against feeling about it—the affective attitude that Margaret Mead says characterizes the Arapesh as contrasted with the more cognitive conception of the universe which I should say characterizes the world view of the Yucatec Maya. The cognitive way of confronting it is necessary, or comes into development, insofar as the world view gets to be expressed informatively, even reflectively. Where there are people who can tell the ethnologist or the historian of their world view, there are people who more than feel about things; they know about them. The movement toward a cosmology may take a variety of forms. Some world views, on their more cosmological side, emphasize existent structure. I think again of the Yucatec Maya, who conceive of a universe that is layered and cornered, oriented to the points of the compass, and provided with a supervisory heaven with seats neatly arranged according to the authority of the occupants. The Arapesh have nothing of the sort. The present-day Maya that I know do not, however, much concern themselves with the origins of things; they have origin myths, but these are unsystematized. The world views of many Polynesian peoples would show us again resemblances and differences. The Maori, for instance, resemble Maya and Zuni as against the Arapesh in that they have knowledge of a structured universe. But in their case the emphasis *is* on the origins; the cosmos is one vast genealogy of procreation and descent from chaos to the person speaking. And this comparison leads off into still other and more special questions as to the cyclical or secular or merely durative character of time in the world view of Maya as compared with that of the Maori, for example.

We might also consider the relation man sees between himself and that which he confronts in terms of what that relation calls upon man to do. World view can be seen as a characteristic attitude of obligation toward that which man finds in his universe. If I read Ruth Bunzel on the Zuni I learn that the duty of man is the performance of those collective rituals that maintain a perpetual and unchanging harmonious oneness of God, man, and nature. The attitude is one of doing one's part in a persistent system. Man helps to keep things running; man does not alter, or destroy, or even obey particular orders. If I read Thorkild Jacobsen on the ancient Mesopotamians, it is this very word "obedience" that I find to be prominent. The gods are powerful; they meet from time to time to take new decisions; the duty of man is to obey the order that comes. Life, to the ancient Mesopotamian but not to the Zuni, is "a pretty arbitrary affair." If I read Daniel Boorstin on the world view of Thomas Jefferson's circle,[14] I find that for them man's part seems to have been to carry out, by changing nature and building institutions, the divine plan so providentially set out by God to be the American's happy destiny in the new continent. Here are at least three distinguishable attitudes toward the Not-Man: to maintain it, to obey it, or to act upon it. No doubt one could find each of these attitudes in each of the three world views, Zuni, Mesopotamian, and early American; but the accounts are persuasive to the conclusion that each of them emphasized one of the three attitudes which the other two did not emphasize.

I return now to the thing confronted and call attention to what seems to me always to be an aspect of that thing: orderliness. Absolute chaos is inconceivable. The notion of regularity, of what is called law, is inescapable. Yet it is probably also true that every world view combines with the idea of law, or regularity, the idea of capriciousness, of what W. G. Sumner called "the aleatory interest." And these ideas of law and capriciousness are probably everywhere connected somehow with ideas of good and evil. Whitehead, who discusses this, writes, "Sometimes the law is good and the capriciousness evil; sometimes the law is iron and the capriciousness is merciful and good. But from savage legends up to Hume's civilized Dialogues on Natural Religion, with the conversations between Job and his friends, the same problem is discussed." [15] The questions might then be asked of a world view: Is the orderliness of the cosmos seen as good, with deviations seen as evil? Are the deviations from law seen as matters of chance, blind and merely happening, or are they seen as intended? These are the questions as to luck and providence. And they lead to the questions on the one hand as to free will and man's power to determine his fate, and on the other as to the presence and character of superhuman volition in the universe.

Whitehead's discussion of cosmologies suggests especially one question that might be asked of world views in
the attempt to understand their significant differences and
similarities. The question is as to the locus of the orderliness of things. If it is true that everywhere people look out
upon a universe with some law in it, some anticipated regularity, the question may be asked: Is the law, the orderliness, inherent in the things, in their very nature; is it
immanent? Or, on the other hand, is it a result of the imposition of order by somebody's will? [16] Whitehead's discussion
is to the effect that until modern times the view of immanence and the view of imposition were variously mixed
in world views. Semitic monotheism inclined toward imposition, Buddhism toward immanence, and Greek thinkers
combined the two conceptions. Thinking of some little-
reported facts as to the world views of primitive peoples,
one is inclined to put forward the view that a common conception among preliterate peoples is that, like Newton,
they think of an orderly system originally set running by
divine will and thereafter exhibiting its immanent order.
Perhaps this view is common among both primitive and
ancient peoples. They see order; they explain the order as
put there by intention. Whether or not they then think of
supernatural will as bound by the order set going is a
question not answered in many accounts of primitive world
view into which I have looked. Perhaps this is a question
to which many primitive peoples do not give attention. The
gods act in their spheres of interest, but whether they do
not or could not stop the sun and moon is not thought about.
On the other hand, my impression is that, in those cases
where the ethnologist has told us how the primitive people
conceive of the relation between divine will and the order
of the universe, the account we get is substantially like

101

that which Kluckhohn gives us for the Navaho, as follows:

Although at the beginning of things certain happenings occurred at the will of the divinities, they themselves were henceforth bound by the consequences of their own acts. Once the machine had been started, it ran according to irreversible laws. There is no place in Navaho thought for the god who can capriciously (from a Navaho point of view) grant the petition of humans.[17]

The mutual involvement of God and nature is, however, pretty plainly a common characteristic of most primitive or ancient world views. Sky and god, rain and deity are somehow together, aspects of the same thing. The radical achievement of the Hebrews in putting God entirely outside of the physical universe and attaching all value to God is recognized as an immense and unique achievement. And the fresh beginning of Greek science in conceiving a universe in which order was immanent without any reference to God at all is also recognized as exceptional and extraordinary. These two tremendous transformations in world view within our own heritage are interestingly described by able scholars of the ancient traditions in the book, *The Intellectual Adventure of Ancient Man.* They are opposite and complementary transformations of earlier world view. The one, by the Hebrews, made God all important. The other, by Greek and modern, made God unnecessary. They are events in the history of world view which depend upon and follow from the advent of civilization. Neither an absolutely unconditioned God nor a wholly secular description of natural law is conceivable in a savage or barbaric settlement before the rise of cities.

Here we come upon another of the great transformations of history. It is one of those transformations which are not apparent if only archaeology is our guide but which come into view when we combine archaeology, ethnology, and history. This transformation is the remaking of the primitive world view by the reflective mind.

To the attempt to conceive the kind of world view which prevailed before the rise of cities, archaeology can provide the merest hints. "It is plain," writes Childe, "that head-hunting, cannibalism, some kind of magic, and even offerings of first-fruits were already practiced by some savages" uninfluenced by more advanced societies.[18] World view, of some sort, is as old as the other things that are equally human and that developed along with world view: culture, human nature, and personality. The archaeological evidences for a confrontation of the universe in religious or magical attitudes is, of course, far richer for the food-producing peoples of the Neolithic and Bronze Ages—one thinks of the temple structures identified by the archaeologists in settlements of the Ubaid period in Mesopotamia, the female figurines or the phalli found in one or another precivilized site, the stone circles of the beaker folk. Before there were cities, there was a view of God and nature and man himself, and an attitude of responsibility to that which man confronted.

But it is through a consideration of the world views of the primitive peoples of present times that we may venture to characterize the generic content of the precivilized world view. Even the few societies which have been mentioned in this chapter will provide us with enough material to support a point or two. Three things may now be said about the world view of precivilized man, and from these things something about the great transformations that have occurred in it.

In the primary condition of humanity man looked out

upon a cosmos partaking at once of the qualities of man, nature, and God. That which man confronted was not three separate things but rather one thing with aspects which, in the light of distinctions that have become much sharper since, we call by these three terms. If later world views might be compared with reference to a triangle of these three conceptions—Man, Nature, God—the primary world view was one in which the triangle itself was not very apparent. This unitary character of the cosmos in the case of the folk peoples is recognized on the one hand when it is said that the world of the folk is pervaded with sacredness. On the other hand, it is recognized when it is said that the world of the folk is personal. The two ideas, put together, refer to the hardly separable interpenetration of man, Nature, and God in that which the precivilized man confronted.

A few paragraphs back I wrote of the involvement of God and nature, so characteristic of primitive and ancient thinking, and of the unique achievement of the Hebrews in ancient times in separating the two. No more need be said here of this aspect of the primary unity. It is the involvement of man and nature that calls for emphasis now. Yet this, too, is an old story in anthropological literature. E. B. Tylor saw that primitive people commonly thought of nature as indwelling spirit, "animistically." R. R. Marett recognized that the attitude toward nature—and men too —is in many cases one of awareness of a less personalized and vaguer power, and wrote of "animatism." Edward Crawley and Ruth Benedict wrote of the treatment of nature as person rather than as thing. Looking at the same facts again, but now with the ancient civilizations also in mind, the Frankforts chose a somewhat different formula: "For modern scientific man the phenomenal world is primarily an 'It'; for ancient—and also for primitive—man it is a 'Thou.' " [19] The Frankforts want us to understand that in this primitive world view the thing confronted is unique; that it is known directly and inarticulately and without detachment; that "it is experienced as life confronting life." [20] As D. D. Lee says, in the primitive world view "man is *in* nature already, and we cannot speak properly of man *and* nature." [21] In this world view there can be no mysticism, because mysticism implies a prior separation of man and nature and an effort to overcome the separation. This primary indistinction of personal, natural, and sacred qualities is the first characteristic to be asserted of the world view of precivilized man.

The second assertion to be made follows from the first. It involves a reconsideration if not actually a recall of that word "confrontation" which I have often used in this discussion. Perhaps we should substitute the word "orientation." For in the primary world view, as nature is not sharply set off as something different from man, the verb "confront" suggests too much a separation that did not so much exist. Being already in nature, man cannot exactly confront it. Primitive man does not, and precivilized man did not, so much set out to "control, or master or exploit." [22] The attitude with which primitive people confront the Not-Man is commonly described as one of placation or appeal or coercion. Others have recognized that this is an inadequate statement of that attitude. The rites of preliterate peoples are also "a formal period of concentrated, enjoyable association." A recent writer says:

The Hopi . . . working on the land, does not set himself in opposition to it. He works *with* the elements, not *against* them. . . . He is in harmony with the elements, not in conflict; and he does not set out to conquer an opponent. He depends on the corn, but this is part of a mutual interdependence; it is not exploitation.[23]

So may we not say that in the primary world view the quality of the attitude toward the Not-Man is one of mutuality? The obligation felt is to do what falls to one in maintaining a whole of which man is part.

The third assertion as to the primary world view here to be made brings us back to a conception introduced in the first chapter, the moral order. In the primary world view Man and Not-Man are bound together in one moral order. The universe is morally significant. It cares. What man sees out there, that which is not himself and yet in which he somehow participates, is a great drama of conduct. Whether it be the spirit-inhabited water hole and the still more important powerful sexuality of his own being, as in the case of the Arapesh, or the rain-gods and maize plants of the Zuni, or the divine authorities of the Mesopotamian invisible state, these entities and dispositions are part of a man-including moral system. The universe is spun of duty and ethical judgment. Even where the Not-Man acts not as man should act, where the supernaturals are unjust or indecent, the conduct of these gods is thought about according to the morality that prevails on earth. The universe is not an indifferent system. It is a system of moral consequence.

So we find that everywhere in the uncivilized societies—and may therefore attribute the characteristic to the precivilized societies also—when man acts practically toward nature, his actions are limited by moral considerations. The attitude of primitive man is mixed, uncertain, to our viewpoint, accustomed as we are to separate purely physical nature toward which we act as expedience suggests. Primitive man is, as I have said, at once in nature and yet acting on it, getting his living, taking from it food and shelter. But as that nature is part of the same moral system in which man and the affairs between men also find themselves, man's actions with regard to nature are limited by notions of inherent, not expediential, rightness. Even the practical, little-animistic Eskimo obey many exacting food taboos. Such taboos, religious restrictions on practical activity, rituals of propitiation or personal adjustments to field or forest, abound in ethnological literature. "All economic activities, such as hunting, gathering fuel, cultivating the land, storing food, assume a relatedness to the encompassing universe." [24] And the relatedness is moral or religious.

The difference between the world view of primitive peoples, in which the universe is seen as morally significant, and that of civilized Western peoples, in which that significance is doubted or is not conceived at all, is well brought out in some investigations that have been made as to the concept of immanent justice in the cases of American Indian children on the one hand and Swiss children on the other. "Immanent justice" is that retribution for my faults which I believe will fall upon me out of the universe, apart from the policeman or a parental spanking. If I do what I know I should not do, will I, crossing the brook, perhaps slip and fall into the water? If I believe this will happen, I live in no indifferent universe; the Not-Man cares about my moral career. Now, when significantly large samples of children were asked questions about this, the results provide some comparisons of interest to us in considering the difference between primitive and modern world view. Of the Swiss children from six to seven years of age, 86 per cent believed in immanent justice. But the older Swiss children began to cease to believe in it; of those from twelve to eighteen years of age only 39 per cent believed. With the Indian children the development was just the other way; of the younger Hopi children 71 per cent, and of the younger Navaho children, 87 per cent believed in immanent justice. Among the older children of both Indian groups (from twelve to eighteen years of age), practically all (87 per cent and 97 per cent) believed in immanent justice. The modern European child begins with a more primitive world view which he corrects to conform to the prevailing adult view. The Indian child begins with a primitive world view which grows stronger with age.[25] Moreover, in the more isolated Navaho community, the belief in immanent justice is stronger than it is in Navaho communities closer to white influence.

If we compare the primary world view that has been sketched in these pages with that which comes to prevail in modern times, especially in the West, where science has been so influential, we may recognize one of the great transformations of the human mind. It is that transformation by which the primitive world view has been overturned. The three characteristics of that view which have been stressed in these pages have weakened or disappeared. Man comes out from the unity of the universe within which he is orientated now as something separate from nature and comes to confront nature as something with physical qualities only, upon which he may work his will. As this happens, the universe loses its moral character and becomes to him indifferent, a system uncaring of man. The existence today of ethical systems and of religions only qualifies this statement; ethics and religion struggle in one way or another to take account of a physical universe indifferent to man.

This transformation stretches over a very great deal of human history. I know nothing of its beginnings in the reflective thought of the Orient. In the primitive societies the basis for the change is already present in the treatment primitive man gives to objects and tools most closely around him in matter-of-fact contexts; the separation of man and the most immediate part of the universe is manifest in much practical action. If I knew more about the histories of thought in the ancient civilizations, I might speak of the slow gathering of this transformation in Egypt or in Mesopotamia. Surely the development of the full-time priestly specialist contributed to it. In primitive societies, as among the village Maya or the ancient rural Roman, the management of man's relationships with the Not-Man was in the hands of everybody, or at least of most of the elder men of the community. As it came into the hands of specialists with increasingly specialized knowledge, this management became more remote from the impulses of ordinary people and more secular.[26] Jacobsen sees in the state-managed rituals of the Mesopotamians evidence for an older view which created these festivals, of a more archaic period in which man "could himself become god, could enter into the identity of the great cosmic forces in the universe which surround him and could thus sway it by action." [27] In this change which Jacobsen sees, we may have a part of the great transformation in world view. The older period he identifies harks back to the primary world view in which man was part of nature and god and acted out his sense of participation. But gradually man comes to stand aside and look first at God-Nature, then, in the case of the Hebrews, God-without-Nature, and then, beginning with the Ionian philosophers "who moved in a curious borderland," [28] at nature without God. The subsequent development of a world view in which God and man are both separated from nature, and in which the

exploitation of material nature comes to be a prime attitude, may be attributable to our Western world almost entirely, and so might be regarded, as Sol Tax has suggested,
as a particular "cultural invention." [29] By the seventeenth
century in European philosophy God was outside the system as its mere clockmaker. To the early American, nature
was God's provision for man's exploitation. I read that it
is Descartes who enunciated the principle that the fullest
exploitation of matter to *any* use is the whole duty of man.
The contemporary Western world, now imitated by the
Orient, tends to regard the relation of man to nature as a
relation of man to physical matter in which application of
physical science to man's material comfort is man's paramount assignment on earth.

V

"Man Makes Himself"

THE title of this chapter is taken—as is much of the stimulation for this little book—from V. Gordon Childe. But the quotation marks around the phrase are also a sign that it is here put to a different use, pushed to a different meaning. In his book with this title Childe writes of the long historical development of tools and institutions wherein man, once a being not yet human, came to be the creature that he is now. The "making of man" with which Childe is concerned is unplanned. It is that making of man in which a future is made that men do not foresee or strive to bring about. The consequences of agriculture and of the building of cities were not intended. They just happened. The institutions in which civilization was founded were, in Sumner's terms, crescive, not enacted. In the early and very much longer part of his history man did not see himself as maker of either his future world or of himself. It is Childe, looking backward upon what happened in history, who sees man as the maker of himself.

On the other hand, in modern civilization as it appears both in the West and in the East, men commonly undertake to make their future world different from the one in which they live. The West invented progress and reform. The East

111

today is in revolt; there is a great purpose to change things. The intentional making over of society is a conception of civilized man, perhaps only of modern man. May we not say that there was no Utopia prior to *The Republic?* But there have been many since, and most of these since the Renaissance. It is true that before Plato the Hebrew prophets looked forward to the building of the Kingdom of God on earth by those few who should be saved from the doom of nations. But the vision of Isaiah, like the visions of Wodziwob, the Paiute Indian prophet of the Second Ghost Dance, and of the prophets of the Vailala Madness of New Guinea, is a dream, a faith, not a plan. Such visions arose out of protests against the consequences of civilization or against the corruption of the traditional folk life. They are, in their nature and function, a link between the myths of primitive peoples and the positive plans of reform of modern peoples. In the throes of moral suffering people create an image of their hopes and fears. But it is at first a mere picture of those hopes and fears. Only later, with the further development of civilization, does the prospective myth become a Utopia and then a plan for action.

In the folk societies men do not seek to make over their own natures. A particular Indian may seek a vision in order to achieve spiritual enlightenment, health, and long life. He is not then considering his own nature as a sort of artifact, a thing to be shaped into a chosen design. Such a conception is not one we are likely to find in a primitive society. We encounter the conception in minds affected by modern science. Listen to an anthropologist, writing a few years ago: "The really serious thing is the kinds of human beings we make." "We are potentially able to shape almost any kind of human personality." To accomplish this, "we need to take an adult, cold-eyed view of our own

112

sacred superegos, our own sacred culture." [1] And the means to the accomplishment of this shaping of human nature, of personality? It is, we are told, the way we bring up our children. Choose the kind of human being you want, recognizing the personal maladjustments or other consequences that will also result, announces this anthropologist, and bring up your children so as to manufacture that kind of person.

Or listen to the distinguished psychiatrist who not long ago declared that the causes of wars lay in morality—no, not in wickedness, or in economic competition, but in the concept of right and wrong itself. Wars might be prevented, he said, by changing men's natures through a change in the content of education. We should, he suggested, "stop imposing our local prejudices and faiths on children and give them all sides of every question so that in their own good time they may have the ability to size things up, and make their own decisions." [2] Such a plan would not occur to primitive man.

Man makes himself, then, in two senses, and the two senses imply a contrast between folk society and, at least, modern civilization. Man is self-made through the slow and unpremeditated growth of culture and civilization. Man later attempts to take control of this process and to direct it where he wills. The contrast suggests a topic and a problem. The topic is the transformation of the folk society into civilization through the appearance and development of the idea of reform, of alteration of human existence, including the alteration of man himself, by deliberate intention and design. The problem is the recognition of the roots of this conception—if any there be—in the primitive societies. It is only the first paragraphs of the story of this revolution in man's condition with which I dare concern myself, with that very little part of it which asks whether in societies primitive or precivilized man is in any significant degree the conscious shaper of his world.

"Reform," "planning," "constitutional amendment" are not categories that we are likely to find employed by an ethnologist reporting the way of life of a primitive society unaffected by civilization. Characteristically he will give us descriptions of customs and institutions, not accounts of people criticizing these customs and institutions, still less trying to create new ones. This may be the case because criticism and creation are not frequent and conspicuous in isolated primitive societies. It may also be because the training of the ethnologist is to record what is usual and institutional, not what is unusual and creatively novel. Where we do find something in an ethnologist's account that seems to represent the primitive people as critical of their own traditions or as reflecting systematically upon them, we may hesitate before accepting it as proof that the primitive people did think critically or philosophically uninfluenced by some representative of modern civilization. Moreover, the ethnologist himself is an influence on the native, and a further influence on the written form given to what the native tells him. In the very attempt to get information he stimulates in his informants a certain amount of reflection and even criticism. And in writing his ethnographic account, the ethnologist tends to put things into an arrangement that is convenient and perhaps esthetically attractive but that may suggest that the average native has a more systematic and reflective view of things than is actually true. All these circumstances reduce to a very small amount the dependable knowledge we have as to the reflective thought and creative action of primitive peoples in their aboriginal conditions.

Let us look first at the evidences for reflective thought in primitive societies. The evidence on which Paul Radin relies in his book *Primitive Man as Philosopher* [3] is subject to the doubt I have mentioned. The Winnebago, and many of the other peoples from whom, directly or indirectly, Radin obtained the texts that indicate skeptical and systematic thinking, were affected by civilization when they told Radin or other students what they doubted or philosophized about. And the texts which Radin puts forward to show primitive skepticism were, in many cases, collected by missionaries. One wonders, for instance, if Bishop Callaway's own presence and activities affected the Amazulu natives who told him that though they thought about Unkulunkulu, their supreme deity, they were aware that none among them really knew about him; they told the Bishop also that they did things that were evil yet justified the doing "since it was made by Unkulunkulu." Few of the materials offered by Radin are perfect proof against the charge that it is a native mind set in motion by a civilized mind that is recorded.

Nevertheless, I think that we must accept the principal conclusion of Radin's book, that in primitive and precivilized societies there is some reflective, critical, and creative thinking. In the twenty-five years since the book appeared, I have seen no important refutation of it and have met a good deal that tends to confirm it. [4] The skepticism reported of the Amazulu about their god and about the predictive value of dreams, a matter which their tradition teaches; the pessimism of the Ba-Ila of Rhodesia who told E. W. Smith and A. M. Dale that their high god, Leza, had "left off doing well"; the Winnebago story of the Indian who openly scoffed at a deity, Disease-Giver, and defied that being to his face to do his worst—some parts of these accounts may be imperfect evidence for the reason I have given. But the cumulative effect is considerable.

The evidence which Radin offers to show that in any primitive society there are some people who make explicit systems out of looser traditional ideas he finds principally in the high degree of systematic arrangement of abstract ideas in the origin myths and cosmological accounts of some primitive peoples. Here, it is the very elaboration of the way in which ideas are related to one another that is the evidence for the existence of the primitive philosopher; one does not actually see him philosophizing; he is inferred from what is taken to be his philosophy. Dr. James Walker reported the conceptions of the Oglala Sioux as to the circle as the basic pattern of the universe and the fundamental symbol of space and time. To this archetypal idea the Indian informant related sun, earth, the year, day, night, the tipi, and the camp circle. Accounts closely corresponding to this, similarly systematizing the universe and many things about man and his acts, I have obtained from Maya Indians of Yucatan; in their case it is the quadrilateral which is the basic and universal pattern. To read Walker's account of the circular universe as described by the Sioux, or the wonderfully complex genealogical systematization of the universe which the Maori priesthood were able to express as reported by Percy Smith and Elsdon Best [5] is to be persuaded that in at least some primitive societies a few people do think about the more general and popular ideas as to the nature of man and the universe and do give these ideas a new depth and consistency. Specialists in the study of the Maori recognize two kinds of cosmogonic myths, a popular form and an esoteric form; the latter, which was secret knowledge of an inner circle of priests, postulated a supreme god hardly known to the ordinary Maori and included episodes of the popular version elaborated with more detail and the introduction of more characters. If a closer view of the operations of the mind of a primitive philosopher is wanted, one may read Marcel Griaule's report [6] of thirty-two long conversations he had with a highly thoughtful and reverent West African native, the blind Dogon tribesman, Ogotemmeli, a man with an extraordinarily comprehensive and detailed world view, reflectively considered and lucidly stated.

To the evidence of such materials, I add my impression that most ethnologists who have worked intimately with isolated, nonliterate people who enjoy even a little time in which one might reflect find in such communities a few people who do reflect. The difference between one native, who acts without much thought, and the occasional native of a reflective and even speculative turn of mind, is apparent to one who has come to know a good many of the adults of a primitive community. Whether or not the intellectual refining of a more general and popular tradition by certain persons who have the time and the inclination to do so is to be called "speculation for its own sake," as Radin calls it, the main point that he makes appears to stick. In primitive as in civilized societies some people live unreflective and matter-of-fact lives, while a few others are disposed to speculation; and these latter accomplish some critical and even creative thought on problems of existence and conduct.

I see no reason to deny the probability that this much creative thinking took place before the first cities were built among some food producers, and even among some food-collecting "savages." The presence of some leisure seems a necessary condition for the first philosophy; we do not find systematic and critical thinking reported from the ever-hungry, frequently tired and sick Bolivian Siriono. The development of a priesthood with a specialized tradition is obviously another favorable precondition. But there seems to be no necessity that the appearance of such thinking had to await full-time specialists. The Andaman Islanders are as much food-collecting savages as are the Siriono, and few more isolated peoples have been studied; yet among them certain men are specialized authorities in the legendary lore, and no less an anthropologist than Boas was willing to declare that if some of these Andamanese "are of philosophic mind, they may adapt the current tales to phenomena of nature and reinterpret them." [7]

Yet the specialized priests of the civilizations certainly greatly advanced such thinking. Systematization and skepticism—these two fruits of the speculative mind are to be found in many a study of the history of thought in the ancient civilizations. An outsider to such studies like myself may refer in this connection to the book entitled *The Intellectual Adventure of Ancient Man*,[8] in which specialists in the study of ancient civilizations tell us of these fruits. There John Wilson [9] explains that the Egyptian inscription known as the Memphite Theology shows the reflective mind working out an adjustment between older and more widely held views as to the origin of the world and the powers of the gods and views appropriate to the rising importance of Memphis. The text, says Wilson, is a theological argument that Ptah, rather than the sun-god, was the primal god, and that Memphis was the center of the world. But more than this, in working out this reinterpretation of religious tradition, the priests of Memphis, says Wilson, subsumed the variant ideas under a higher philosophy. In place of the older idea of the creation of the world in such physical terms as, say, the Maori also conceived it, as separation of earth from sky, these Egyptian priests related creation to the processes of thought and speech and so anticipated the Book of Genesis.

In the same book, Thorkild Jacobsen's interesting discussion [10] of the Gilgamesh epic shows systematization and also growing skepticism among the ancient Mesopotamians. This epic Jacobsen finds was composed around the beginning of the second millennium before Christ out of older stories woven into a new whole. It is a work of synthesis, of reflective adjustment of parts to make a work philosophically coherent. The later work is no mere chronicle of primitive creation, episode by episode. Its theme is death, and it asks the great question as to why the good must die. A later Mesopotamian document, known as "The Dialogue of Pessimism," foreshadows Ecclesiastes, for in this ancient composition love, charity, and piety are one by one examined and found empty; the conclusion is reached that good and evil alike will be forgotten and so be indistinguishable. This is a development of speculative thought, hinted at only in the words of the African native or the Sioux Indian, but now, in an ancient civilization, carried far forward in the direction of a skeptical philosophy. These examples are enough to remind us that civilization is the cultivation of our more ultimate purposes. By the folk the moral order is, on the whole, taken as given. There only a few people are able to ask the great questions, or can look with doubt and intellectual challenge at what is for most men all of the time taken for granted; and, without writing, what these few minds accomplish leaves little residue. But the first cities bring a literate elite and a new freedom of the mind to criticize and to record. Then the moral order, though it is shaken by civilization, is also, in civilization, taken by reason into charge.

The moral order in early civilization is taken in charge by specialists as a philosophical problem. But this is not to say that it is taken in charge as a program for action. The little sketch of the development of the speculative mind which I have given brings us to a freer and more creative kind of thinking than could have existed in precivilized societies. It does not show us man undertaking to change his world and himself. Let us return to the societies known to ethnologists for what light they may shed on reform in the human community before the first civilizations.

The important statement that is generally true and relevant here is that in primitive societies uninfluenced by civilization the future is seen as a reproduction of the immediate past. Men see their children doing on the whole what they did themselves and are satisfied to see them doing so. The fortunes of individual men and women may rise or fall; calamity may strike one man or everybody, and success may or may not come; but the ways of life, the things to try for and to realize, remain the same.

The point is made plainer when one looks at the institutions by which civilized men sometimes seek to change their world to see whether or not these same institutions are used for such a purpose in primitive societies. The answer is, of course, that they are not. Consider education, and consider what the sociologist calls "voluntary associations." These two institutions have for their function in primitive societies—and hence, I am asserting, in precivilized societies—the reproduction of the current mode of life. They do not, as in our own society, take on also the function of changing the current mode of life in some direction of intended change.

It is now abundantly demonstrated that in many a primitive society there is education in the sense of conscious

120

effort of adults to influence the behavior of children and younger people in directions which the adults think desirable. The direction is a repetition of the adults' way of life. Studies of primitive education which I have read [11] make other points about that education: that moral instruction is its core; that it sometimes strives to recognize special abilities of individuals and is modified to fit; that the techniques of instruction are often well adapted to their ends. But it may be safely said that during all of human history until recent times the end of education has been to make, by education, the sort of adult that is admired in the society in which the teacher himself grew up and to make the child ready for a world like that in which the teacher lives. Margaret Mead has put the contrast between primitive education and modern Western education so clearly that I can do no better than to quote her words.

Primitive education was a process by which continuity was maintained between parents and children. . . . Modern education includes a heavy emphasis upon the function of education to create discontinuities—to turn the child of the peasant into a clerk, the farmer into a lawyer, of the Italian immigrant into an American, of the illiterate into the literate.[12]

And also: "Education becomes a mechanism of change." The belief has grown up in America "that it was possible by education to build a new world—a world that no man had yet dreamed . . . that we can bring up our children . . . to be equipped as we never were equipped." [13] Nor does Dr. Mead neglect to mention the conflicts that result in our kind of civilized society between the more popular and widespread desire to use education to keep things as they are, and the desire of some modern people to build a new and better world with it. This very new dimension of education is a development of modern civilization. I do not know if the disposition to change society by changing one's children appears at all in the ancient civilizations; I should doubt it. Here we are talking of one of the later aspects of what perhaps we might speak of as the transforming advent of reform.

Nor shall we find the beginnings of reform in the secret societies and other associations of the primitive peoples. These institutions, like the education of the children, function to maintain the social system, to carry on established values. The medicine societies of the Western Pueblos,[14] the secret societies of Oceania,[15] and those of the Omaha Indians [16]—in the accounts of these I read how the associations fulfill personal needs or societal functions that help to integrate society. Or, if we read how the secret societies, or soldier's bands, contribute toward social change, we find that the social change occurred without the intention of those who took part in it. R. H. Lowie,[17] and K. Llewellyn and E. A. Hoebel [18] have shown us how the Plains Indian soldier societies on the one hand distributed authority among groups that crosscut one another, and how on the other, they made possible a growing centralization of tribal authority. But this is only social change; it is not a program of reform. The most that the ethnographic materials suggest as to the possible relation of associations to the idea of reform is that from a conflict of interests within a primitive society the purposes of one group in its struggle for power with another might have stimulated the formulation of programs of action. Ralph Linton [19] tells us that after the Comanche Indians moved out onto the Plains, the young men of the tribe, organized into age grades with strong *esprit de corps*, exhibited marked disrespect of their elders. Perhaps out of such conflict a struggle for authority might develop which would make the young men and the old men two contending factions within the society. And a faction is a political group, a group that commonly develops a plan and a policy. But this is speculation; I find no real evidence that it happened among the Comanche. I think that if we are to look for the development of explicit programs of social change in precivilized societies, it is in these situations of conflicting special interest that we are likely to find it, if at all. Primitive societies are certainly not altogether static; changing environmental circumstances, meetings with other peoples, and the very variety of viewpoint and interest which exists even in a small homogeneous group are factors that stimulate change. But we are here not looking for the roots of social change; we seek the origins of the concept of reform.

On the whole, I think that neither the primitive societies nor the ancient civilized societies show us, except rarely, the phenomenon of conscious reform in their institutions. It is not easy for men to adopt the explicit position that it is their work to make over human living. Ancient reformers speak as if they were restoring the purity of the past. An announced purpose to change things in such a way as to make a society different from what had ever been before is probably unimportant in Western history until quite modern times, and even there begins gradually, with the writing of Utopias, the fanciful projection of alternative states of society, and reorganizations of society after periods of war or other disorder. In China, where the mode of life was relatively so self-contained for so long, the revolutionary purpose, except for the Ch'in period, is not to be noted until very recent times. Even in modern civilized societies most of the associations which men and women join exist to carry on some function, or realize some interest that on the whole maintains the existing state of affairs. The associations which the Lynds described for Middletown [20] are of this sort—women's clubs and men's business associations, lodges, and all the rest. On the other hand, it is plain that as compared with the associations of primitive people, the element of "conscious manipulation and control" [21] plays a larger part in the associations of Middletown; and, furthermore, organizations with the full intention of changing society in important respects, for the general interest of everybody come into existence in civilization. Especially in the United States, reform has a lively history, and American reforming associations include such groups as the Association for Calendar Reform, the Committee to Repeal the McCarran Act, the religious missions, and the United World Federalists.

I say again that in primitive and in precivilized societies, the minds of men look to a future that reproduces the immediate past. Yet in a time of great crisis the minds of men imagine a future that is different from the past. Reform has two parts: a vision of an altered future, and a program for reaching it. It is the vision, the dream, that comes easier to a people. It takes longer in the human career for people to formulate and adopt programs of reforming action.

The dream we see in the transformation of mythology which happens when a homogeneous and little-changing society meets its crisis. The common crisis is that which is brought upon the primitive society by the impact of civilization. The story of the transformation of mythology from its original primitive form, in which the vision is backward, to a form characteristic of crisis and change and of civilization, in which the vision is forward, is an important part of the story of Utopias and of planning for reform.

In any anthropologist's account of mythology we are

sure to find mythology identified with stories of what has happened. "Mythological concepts are the fundamental views of the constitution of the world and of its origin," wrote Boas.[22] And, recognizing the same justification of experience and of action which Bronislaw Malinowski sees in the mythology of primitive peoples, Boas points out the common presence in such mythologies of "the idea that what happened once has determined the fate of the world." [23] For it is true that the sacred stories of undisturbed primitive peoples, this "pragmatic charter," as Malinowski calls it,[24] is a guide to and validation of action always with regard to something which was, to some event in the past. If one turns from Boas and Malinowski, writing of the myths of primitives, to Sorel, writing of the myths of the parties and classes of modern civilization, one finds the same understanding of the nature of myth, the myth judged "as a means of acting on the present." [25] "A myth cannot be refuted," writes Sorel, "since it is, at bottom, identical with the convictions of the group." [26] But there is an important contrast: the myths of which Sorel writes are stories of things that have never yet happened but are to happen in the future. The myth of the returning Messiah, the coming of the Kingdom of Heaven, the dreams of Luther and Calvin of Christian renovation, and the Marxian myth of the general strike are myths that guide men, not to reproduce in the future the conduct of the past, as is true with the myths of primitive peoples, but to shape a future that will be different from the past. They are revolutionary myths, myths of the overturn of the established order. These myths of which Georges Sorel writes are all myths of civilized peoples, expressive of a period of creativity, of dynamism. "Mankind is once more on the move." [27]

It is the contact and conflict of differing traditions that

brings about the sudden alterations in society and, among other consequences, the change from a mythology that is retrospective to one that is prospective. Sometimes the mythology of the past contains within it the sleeping germ of a prospective mythology. The idea that Quetzalcoatl might some day return was, I suppose, somewhere within the great culture myth of the Nahua peoples of ancient Mexico; the idea rose to current importance when Quetzalcoatl, in the person of the Spaniards, did apparently return. The Yucatecan Maya of the isolated villages told me that an ancient race, pale-skinned builders of the great shrine cities, slept beneath the ground. When the American archaeologists arrived, the story was told me again, but now with the suggestion that the ancient race had arisen from its long sleep and—this was the forward turning of the ancient tale—would now guide the village Indians into a new world of progress and enlightenment.

In each of the nativistic movements among Indian or Oceanic peoples we find a prospective mythology. Mankind is on the move again, or is urged to be on the move, by leaders who now preach a new cult, a new and coming event. A ship will arrive with the spirits of the dead; the bison will return; the end of the world will come. In the course of these movements the people turn in some degree away from the leaders of the old and traditional ways of life to these preachers of new cults. "Mimesis is directed toward creative personalities who command a following because they are pioneers." [28]

In the cults of these primitive folk, on the margins of the white man's civilized world, however, the creative movement is rarely carried very far forward. The return of the old conditions of life is a part of the nativistic myth; the vision of the future is a new path to follow back again into the past. After a great impending catastrophe, prophesied the Paiute Indian leaders of the Ghost Dance, the Indians that had died would return to earth and the land would pass from control of the white man back again to the Indian. The early prophets who in New Guinea led the movement known as the Vailala Madness told their followers that a ship would come bringing back to New Guinea the people's deceased relatives and bearing rifles with which the white man would be driven from Papua. But in the great myths of recent civilized peoples, the myths of which Sorel was thinking, the core and body of the tale is the account of a society that never was and yet is one day to be, a striking forward into the millennium, into the time when the lion and the lamb shall lie down together, the Kingdom of God be realized on earth, or each shall take according to his need and give according to his ability. The spirit of reform, the making of man's world by man's design, which makes civilization so different a thing from precivilized living, begins with the dreaming of the great revolutionary dreams.

Does it also begin in an immediate act? May we find, in primitive society, man not as a dreamer of a new world, but man as a pragmatic reformer, man exerting himself here and now to change the world around him nearer to his desires?

It is clear that in the early civilizations, where a variety of ideas and views of life are brought into competitive stimulation of one another, and where power is gathered into the hands of a single ruler, sweeping reforms may be at least attempted. One thinks again of the attempt of Amenhotep IV (Akhnaton) to impose on Egypt the cult of Aton, and of the burning of the Confucian books under Shih Huang Ti. And, on the side of the common people, civilization provides at least that discontent that may generate reform; strikes of workers and rebellions of subject peoples were certainly not unknown in the ancient civilizations. But we are just now looking at the peoples never civilized to see if we can find among them that essentially civilized and especially modern type, the reformer.

The abolition of the ancient taboos in Hawaii in the year 1819 [29] was certainly a sweeping reform, and it occurred among people who were not, in the usual sense, civilized. The event was, to most of the Hawaiian people, far from gradual; it was catastrophic. One day, in sight of the people, the ladies of the royal family ate forbidden foods, and then —abomination to the old gods—the king came over and ate publicly with the women. So drastic a violation of sacred custom was this that the people realized, however they felt about it, that the taboos were permanently broken and the old gods overthrown. The high priest himself destroyed his temple.

Were Kaahumanu and her fellow conspirators reformers? It seems plain that they were. They intended to overthrow a system both religious and political, and they accomplished their end. But when we ask if the reform would have been even attempted had the civilization of the white man not come into the South Seas, we ask a question that is unanswerable but that raises doubts that the reform would have then been attempted in the absence of influences from civilization. Although the event occurred five months before the first Christian missionaries landed, the Hawaiians for forty years had been getting—and appreciating—the weapons, cloth, and other material goods of the white man. Kamehameha I had two trusted white advisors. The first missionaries to arrive in Hawaii were received by royal ladies dressed in European style. Liholiho, the ruling chief at that time, was already living in a European kind of house. He and his father had built his conquests with European weapons and European advice. Ship captains had had to fight off bold young Hawaiians who were eager to join the crew and see the world. There is evidence that the Hawaiians had heard of the overthrow of native religion already accomplished in Tahiti.[30] Before the missionaries reached Hawaii, two Hawaiians who were not "taboo chiefs" had had themselves baptized Christians by the chaplain of a French ship. So it is quite plain that the prestige of the white man and even of his religion had affected Hawaiians before the overthrow of the taboo. Moreover, the introduction of the white man's weapons had intensified the struggles between family groups, some of which were antitaboo, and the new trade in sandalwood had placed new strains on the social and political system. These are all elements in the situation which suggest that influence from the whites brought about the great reform. On the other hand, the native mode of life included some features, apart from white influence, which plainly made it easier for this reform to succeed should it be attempted. Among these features were the inconsistency between the high position of certain women in the system of political power and the low position of these women as women, as expressed in the taboos; the habituation of the Hawaiians, like other Polynesians, to the desertion of their gods; "the acceptance of a more powerful god as a means of obtaining spiritual power was a common Polynesian characteristic"; and, of course, the personal interests that those disadvantaged by the taboo system had in doing away with it. Kroeber's view [31] that the main factor was "a kind of social staleness," that the Hawaiians were simply tired of their religion, may be right; but such an interpretation has to

129

be considered together with the evidence that young Hawaiians, stimulated by white contacts and new opportunities to travel and trade, were inclined to try the new as much as to give up the old. The strict conclusion is that this Hawaiian reform is not a case of a reform accomplished quite outside of or before civilization. It occurred on the margins of the expanding white man's civilization. It took place among a people whose primitive mode of life included, in addition to the elements favoring change that I have already mentioned, one of the elements which in civilized societies helps to make reform achievable, marked concentration of political power.

In the same year in which these Hawaiian leaders overthrew their traditional religion and system of taboos, or perhaps in the year preceding (1818), there took place in what is now Nebraska an act of reform that is more securely to be credited to the unsupported initiative of certain primitive and precivilized individuals. The event is recorded in James' and Bell's accounts of S. H. Long's expedition.[32] We cannot tell from these accounts just what eyewitnesses of the event reported just what facts to these early travelers into our West; some of the story was told them by traders who had preceded them, but it is almost certain that some of the details were told to James and Bell by the Pawnee Indians themselves. And, at their coming a year or two after the event, the central figure in the episode was personally presented to these white men. This was Petalesharoo, son of Knife Chief of the Loup (or Skidi) [33] band of the Pawnee.

By ancient custom, this group of Pawnee each year sacrificed a captive to Venus, Morning Star, to ensure abundant crops. The victim, fattened and kept uninformed of the fate ahead, was on the proper day bound to a cross or

130

scaffold, tomahawked, and shot with arrows. For several years Knife Chief "had regarded this sacrifice as an unnecessary and cruel exhibition of power, exercised upon unfortunate and defenseless individuals whom they were bound to protect; and he vainly endeavored to abolish it by philanthropic admonitions." [34]

A young girl from another tribe was brought captive to the Pawnee village in the year before, or the second year before, the arrival of Long's party. She was bound to the cross when Knife Chief's son stepped forward "and in a hurried but firm manner, declared that it was his father's wish to abolish this sacrifice; that for himself, he had presented himself before them, for the purpose of laying down his life upon the spot, or of releasing his victim." [35] He then cut the victim's cords, put her on a horse, mounted another, and carried her to safety.

The importance of this occurrence in indicating that in a primitive society a courageous individual may act against the convictions of his own people, against the moral order of his own group, is the more plainly seen when it is understood that in this case the reformer did indeed fly in the face of the opinion of his public. There is little or nothing in the accounts to show that a Christian or humanitarian influence from white people had stimulated the young Pawnee to act as he did. Apparently at this time these Indians had had contact, but not very intimate contact, with a few traders, appearing singly among the Indians. It cannot be denied that it is possible that advice given by a trader may have moved Knife Chief to take the stand which he took and which was then taken also by his son. There is nothing in the accounts we have to show that this happened. What the accounts do show, however, is that this father and his son stood against the overwhelming sentiments of their own people. This was not a case where the common opinion had changed, and people had become ready for reform. For, probably in the year following Petale-sharoo's act, another captive was made ready for sacrifice again, and again Knife Chief and his son tried to rescue the captive, in this case a Spanish boy. On this occasion a trader was present in the village, and Knife Chief, with manufactured goods obtained from this trader, bought the boy from the Indian who had been his captor, and saved his life. James' account does not suggest that the trader took any active part in this second episode until approached by Knife Chief. Nor did this second attempt to end the custom succeed in doing so, for in John T. Irving's account [36] of a visit to these same Pawnee made in 1822, we read that one Major Dougherty was summoned to the Loup Pawnee village to save a young Indian woman whom the Pawnee were about to sacrifice. Again it was the chief who showed himself favorable to saving the prisoner. (Was this chief again Petalesharoo's father? Irving's account refers to "Black Chief.") The other Indians were determined to perform the sacrifice. And so firm was the general opinion still, in spite of these three attempts by the chief to stop the custom, that when Major Dougherty and his white companions, with the aid of the chief, tried to carry off the captive, the Indians slew her with arrows. So the original attempt of Petalesharoo to rescue the captive of that year's ceremony was made against a general will to perform the sacrifice which withstood two more attempts to put an end to it in subsequent years. That this young Indian dared to act so boldly against the wishes of his people remains remarkable, even after we have allowed for the fact that he had the support of his father (or perhaps of his mother's brother—these Pawnee were matrilinear) and that therefore as distinguished warrior and successor of the chief he was a distinguished person. The other fact that seems of major significance in helping us to understand the event is that these Pawnee practiced human sacrifice while none of the other Indian groups around them did so. Speculation suggests that it might have been the contrast between their own custom, in slaying a defenseless person as an offering, and the absence of the custom everywhere else in the world the Pawnee knew, that suggested the reform.

These facts and ideas hardly arrange themselves into a clear portrayal of the primitive reformer. The knowledge we have of creative and original thought and act, in the primitive societies before we, the white missionary or anthropologist, got there is very little. The facts that bear on the question that has been here brought forward throw only a glimmer of light on the roots of reform in precivilized society.

The strongest impression is that in societies unaffected by civilization men change their ideas and their ways of doing things, and are not infrequently aware that they are doing so, but that under conditions of isolation these changes are small changes. The reach into the future to make life different from what it was is a short reach. And the reach occurs when some immediate circumstances present the people with a difficulty. It cannot be proved that the systematization of ideas in Polynesian or Sioux mythology came about by a series of small modifications suggested by differences in versions known of the same traditional myth, but it seems to me probable that this is the way most of the systematization occurred. Most of the changes in making rules for the conduct of a simple society probably occurred also in the course of meeting particular new situations in which the old rules could not be simply applied. There is much material on such altering of the rules in that exceedingly interesting book about the law-ways of the early Cheyenne Indians written by Llewellyn and Hoebel.[37] There we read accounts of such events, occurring before white contact, as the following:

1) According to Cheyenne custom, a man might borrow something he needed even in the absence of the owner provided he left some article of his own as security. But then the Cheyenne acquired horses (from other Indians). A Cheyenne borrowed another man's horse, leaving his bow as security. After a year he had not yet returned the horse. The Elk Soldiers, one of the Cheyenne military societies, on application of the owner of the horse, got it back for him and in doing so promulgated a modification of the old rule: thereafter there was to be no more borrowing of horses without asking permission.

2) One Walking Rabbit ran off with another man's wife and turned up in a war party which he was expected to join. The warriors delayed their military expedition while they deliberated on what to do and agreed to send Walking Rabbit back with the woman and to give horses to the aggrieved husband. But when Walking Rabbit got back to camp, the affair had been ended through his father who had already made a settlement with the woman's husband. Then the Cheyenne discussed the case and reached the conscious decision that thereafter war parties were not to have authority to act with regard to matters of divorce and remarriage.

In these and other cases, Llewellyn and Hoebel show us that there is legislation in primitive societies. They also show, more generally, that even before the rise of civilization men are well aware of conflicting norms, of uncertainties of principle or policy, and, within limits that result in some but not much modification of their ways of life, make conscious decisions of change.

In both thinking and acting, precivilized man carried on, we may infer, a life of choice and doubt, and made formulations of ideas or decisions governing future action which were original and creative. If we had been in such a precivilized society we should have recognized men with minds like ours and men conscious that they had some control of their destinies. Indeed, in spite of the much greater development of conceptions of reform and progress in modern times, I am not sure it can be said that most modern men feel more in control of their destinies than did those Cheyenne Indians.

On the other hand, to recognize this common humanity of problem-seeing and problem-solving is not to say that primitive man was conspicuously a reformer. Of course he was not. Until the coming of civilization men were used to expecting the future to be like what they had themselves experienced, and their institutions kept things running; they did not exist to make life over.

But the human nature was the same, and men in primitive societies can readily turn to the future and conceive it to be made different from the past, if events require that they do so. The turning of the prospective myth forward in a crisis, at a time when the old ways of life are broken and have become unserviceable, shows that this is so. I was myself struck with the rapidity with which certain Maya Indians living in isolated villages in Yucatan adopted the idea of reform, the notion that they would make over at least the material conditions of their lives, when the spirit of the Mexican revolution of 1917–1921 reached them far out in the bush. Where the fathers in the home community had conserved ancient tradition, the sons, out in a new settlement, decided, very conscious of what they were doing, to build a healthier and more prosperous life.[38] Progress is rapidly contagious. There is nothing in the natural capacities of primitive people to prevent them from taking the idea almost instantly.

It is plain that civilization provides the circumstances in which these capacities to build a new future are demanded and so come into development. Civilization is breakdown of old ways. It is a meeting of many minds. It is the weight of new exactions upon human labor; and it is the organization and mass production of food, buildings, war, cruelty, and political adventure. The reformer is not likely to arise nor to be welcomed in a society where everybody does much the same thing and young people go on doing what old people did. The reformer, in Professor Schlesinger's apt phrase is "a disturber of the peace." [39] But what if the peace is already disturbed? It is always disturbed, for many people, in civilization. Then the reformer strives to change the world, already so troubled, or to change the people in it.

Primitive people are potential but not actual reformers. But then I remember Petalesharoo, the young Pawnee. He was actual. He is there, a puzzle and a hint of human goodness. To his fellow tribesmen he must very much have been a disturber of the peace. He was a pacifist, a subversive character. How did he get that way? If only we knew. Did he and his father (or maternal uncle) look about them beyond the members of their own band to those other Indians, some of them Pawnee like themselves, of similar customs and language, who practiced no human sacrifice, and so contrasted the idea of compassion, of tenderness to the helpless, with the girl on the scaffold and the lifted tomahawk? "The history of reform," says Emerson, "is always identical, it is the comparison of the idea with the fact." [40] Was it this contrast, in this case emphasized in the contrast between the customs of his own people and those of other people, that made Petalesharoo a reformer?

It is unfortunate that we do not know and can hardly hope to find out how it was that these Skidi Pawnee came to practice human sacrifice in the first place. The answer that is likely to be given by an anthropologist, based on no direct evidence as to the facts in this particular case, is that the ancestors of these Pawnee learned such a custom in the course of association with Mexican Indians or with some intermediate people who practiced it. Speculating about these matters, one wonders how a people learn to practice a cruelty that they did not practice before. One wonders if such a custom is adopted suddenly. Are there in primitive societies revolutions to introduce human sacrifice and torture? Or are such cruelties developed slowly out of earlier smaller cruelties? Did the Pawnee begin by sacrificing other things and so come, step by step, to sacrifice human beings? Are evils characteristically developed by degrees, but virtues occasionally adopted by sudden reform? When the reformer appears, and is moved to risk his life on a sudden break with the past against public opinion, does he characteristically do so on the side of moral change which the later verdict of history regards as an advance? Or are there also reformers against the historical trend of moral change? Petalesharoo's case suggests the possibility that the reformer is characteristically on the side that history comes to approve. Even Hitler did not preach man's inhumanity to man; he just acted it. And Petalesharoo has been followed by many others who carried on his work and who have declared, throughout more civilized centuries, the generous and humane doctrine which his deed implied. Perhaps Petalesharoo is one of those who before civilization had come to him caught the great idea in history of which Whitehead wrote, the idea of man's humanity to man, and acted out that idea to his own danger and against his own people and his own compelling tradition.

V I

The Transformation of
Ethical Judgment

IN THIS last chapter I will consider some of the questions
that arise when we look at the primitive or the precivilized
cultures with a view to the goodness or the badness of
them. If my reader has borne with me thus far, there is an
acquaintance between us of which I shall take advantage.
I shall write in a vein somewhat more personal than I have
used before. My own behavior, as an anthropologist, is
relevant to the subject now to be discussed, for I am interested here in the way anthropologists do or do not place
values on the things they see in prehistoric or in contemporary nonliterate or illiterate societies, and what comes
of it if they do. I shall venture to anthropologize the anthropologists, and shall not leave myself out of their number.

At the end of the last chapter, writing of Petalesharoo,
the Pawnee Indian who in the face of the customs of his
tribe rescued a woman prisoner about to be put to death
ceremonially and strove to end human sacrifice among his
people, I called him "a hint of human goodness." Plainly
I placed a value on his conduct. Looking back twenty-five
years, I recall when as a student I first heard the story of
Petalesharoo from Professor Fay-Cooper Cole, anthropol-

ogist. He told the story with great human warmth, and I know that then I responded sympathetically. Now I begin to wonder if he or I *could* tell the tale barely, neutrally, without implying admiration of the deed.

In the course of these pages, I have not infrequently indicated my admiration for some act, my approval of some turn in human events. The long story of human affairs which I have been sketchily recounting is a story in which I have not pretended to be disinterested. It is the human biography; it is your story and mine; how can we help but care? I have not tried to conceal a certain sense of satisfaction that in the childhood of our race, before there were cities, precivilized men, like the preliterates of today, recognized moral obligations, even if the moral rules were not my rules. I think this better than the unrestrained selfishness which Hobbes imagined wrongly to characterize the behavior of men before political society developed. So when in the course of these discussions I have encountered in some uncivilized society a custom which I liked or disliked, I think I have in many cases shown how I felt about it. I regret that the Siriono in the Bolivian forest abandon their dying kinsmen without a word, while I come to understand the rigors of their life that make such conduct excusable. I am pleased that the Yagua in their big communal houses respect even a child's desire to be alone, and refrain from speaking to him when he turns his face to the wall. When I came to the change in human living that was brought about through the food-producing and the urban revolutions, I am sure that I showed a certain sense of anxiety as to how humanity would manage to live well under the new conditions, so disruptive of the old arrangements for moral life. I gloried in the rise of creative intelligence, as represented in systematic philosophic thought and in the world religions. I simply could not look neutrally at the ideas that move in history toward a more humane ideal and practice.

This is, perhaps, a shocking admission. What right have I, who admit to caring about the human career, to speak as an anthropologist? For are not anthropologists enjoined to adopt in their work a rigid objectivity? Professor Kroeber has written that "there is no room in anthropology for a shred of ethnocentricity, of homino-centricity." [1] My ethnocentricity appears in the positive valuations I have placed on the increase and widening of humane standards, for are not such standards a special pride of Euro-American civilization? And my homini-centricity is patent: I have placed myself squarely on the side of mankind, and have not shamed to wish mankind well.

My predicament stimulates an examination of some of the problems of objectivity and value judgment that arise in anthropology. There are a good many of these problems, and I shall try to sort them out and to reach at least the first points of understanding as to what is involved in some of them.

Two of these questions I at once set aside as outside consideration at the moment, the one because today it is not much contested, and the other because it is too fundamental for my powers and belongs to the philosophers. As to the first, it is recognized that values are a proper subject matter of anthropology. Indeed, value studies are something of a fashion among faculties of anthropologists, who sometimes join in this work with sociologists and indeed with philosophers. Here it is other people's values that the anthropologist sets out to study. His questions are: What is a value? How do you find out about it? [2] It is not much doubted that it is proper and possible for anthropologists to make valid assertions about other people's conceptions as to the desirable.

The question from which anthropologists turn aside is the problem of the metaphysical locus of the good, with the problem of the nature or content of the intrinsic good. As to this I think a decision characteristic of anthropology has been recently expressed by Professor Firth:

The anthropologist . . . is not concerned directly with questions of ethics—the abstract, philosophical examination of the bases of right and wrong in general, the assumptions on which such notions are founded, the problem of the existence of intrinsic good and evil, and their relation to human conduct and destiny.[3]

Most anthropologists would accept that as their position.

The problems, in the field of morality, with which Professor Firth *is* concerned are two. One is to understand particular moralities. The anthropologist tries to understand what it is that a people conceive to be desirable. And he tries to understand how these conceptions are related to other things about that people—to the way in which status is distributed conventionally among them, for instance.

There is a growing tendency, which Professor Firth also recognizes, for anthropologists to be concerned with a second problem, one which they conceive as both possible and remote of solution. This is the effort to find out what moral principles are universal because universal conditions of human living give rise to them. Firth mentions regulation and restraint in sexual affairs, stability of human sex relations sufficient to allow for the minimum care for infants, and some curbs on violence within the group. "As some factors are discernible in the basic requirements of all societies, so certain moral absolutes exist." [4] Professor

142

Kluckhohn, too, claims this second problem as an anthropological enterprise. He too names some of the values which are probably universal. He adds the idea that as "new knowledge of radically changed circumstances may alter universal values . . . one might speak of 'conditional absolutes.'"[5] Perhaps Professor Kluckhohn was thinking of Orwell's *1984;* it might be possible, by an evil sort of conditioning, to put dehumanized creatures inside our skins.

These kinds of concerns with values are, then, proper to anthropologists. We look at other people, and find out what they value and how this valuing works out in their cases. And we hope to find out what conceptions as to the desirable are characteristic of all of mankind, at least "so far," because the conditions of living, in families, neighborhood groups, and so forth, have been, for all the local differences, in certain general respects the same.

The questions about values as to which the anthropologically correct answer is less clear are those which have to do with valuing when it is done by the anthropologists themselves. What valuing is proper to an anthropologist, and how does he properly reach a valuation? Of course we are here thinking of the anthropologist in his professional, his scientific, capacity. As I shall say later, I am not sure I can tell where his scientific capacity ends and where begins his disposition as a human being to place values on things. But just now I will assume that it is possible to ask of him, as anthropologist, a sharply distinguishable kind of behavior with respect to valuing.

The anthropologists have, on the whole, considered the question as asking if their scientific methods are applicable to questions about whether something is better than something else. Not being theistic theologians, they have not asked if the intrinsic good can be determined by consulting the revelations of God, and not being philosophers, they have not sought a rational demonstration, resting on common knowledge alone, that one way of thought or action is better than another. They have found that the way they use their minds in coming to a conclusion as to what kind of pottery people make or what kind of values these other people, not anthropologists, place on cannibalism or on chastity does not work when they are asked to establish that one value is better for a man to hold than another. And they have not experienced much trouble in distinguishing fact statements from value statements. The former only, they are sure, are their business.

Since Westermarck wrote two books to show that it is not possible to establish one way of thought or action as better than another, if not before that time, anthropologists have taken this position. It has come to have a name: cultural relativism. Most anthropologists would, I think, accept the term as naming their position, or would take the position without perhaps accepting the name. Cultural relativism means that the values expressed in any culture are to be both understood and themselves valued only according to the way the people who carry that culture see things. In looking at a polygamous society and a monogamous society, we have no valid way to assert that the one is better than the other. Both systems provide for human needs; each has values discoverable only when we look at marriage from the point of view of the man who lives under the one system or the other. This is, necessarily then, also to be said in comparing cultures which practice torture, infanticide, in-group sorcery, and homosexuality with those that do not. The gist of cultural relativism as stated by Professor Herskovits, who has discussed the concept at length,[6] is that "judgments are based on experience, and experience is interpreted by each individual in terms of his own enculturation."[7]

With this proposition I do not disagree. I fail to see that having accepted it one finds it necessary to accept everything else that Professor Herskovits says about cultural relativism. It is possible, I think, to agree that everybody passes judgments as guided by the experience he was brought up to have and recognize, and yet to assert some reasonable basis for preferring one thought or action to another. Eliseo Vivas has recently pointed out [8] some ambiguities and difficulties in maintaining the principle, as Professor Herskovits has stated it, and himself concludes, contrary to the principle, that it *is* possible to establish such a better or a worse, because just as corrections of value judgments take place within a society, and within an individual, as action is compared with ideals, so corrections can be made cross-culturally, the corrections being guided by conceptions as to what men ought to be.

However this may be, I am persuaded that cultural relativism is in for some difficult times. Anthropologists are likely to find the doctrine a hard one to maintain. The criticisms of philosophers will be directed more sharply against it. Moreover, the experiences of anthropologists are changing, and these changed experiences will work changes in their judgments as to the relativity of values. (It occurs to me that this proposition is itself an application of the principle!) It was easy to look with equal benevolence upon all sorts of value systems so long as the values were those of unimportant little people remote from our own concerns. But the equal benevolence is harder to maintain when one is asked to anthropologize the Nazis, or to help a Point Four administrator decide what to do for those people he is committed to help. The Point Four man is committed to do something to change that people, for he cannot help them without changing them, and what is the anthropologist to say when the Point Four man asks him just what he ought to do? Perhaps the anthropologist can keep on saying: "Do A, and X will result, but Y will result from doing B—*you* choose which to do." But I doubt that if the anthropologist says only this, he and the administrator will get on very well together. And perhaps the anthropologist, if he continues this neutrality, and yet sees a smash coming, will be just a little restless at night.

At any rate, I should like to point out that the doctrine of cultural relativism does enjoin the benevolence. It is a doctrine of ethical neutralism, but it is not a doctrine of ethical indifference. Ruth Benedict's *Patterns of Culture* is an exemplification of cultural relativism. She wrote in large part to tell us that all cultures are "equally valid." But this meant, for her, not that we are to value none of them, but that we are to value all of them. The book is a call to positive sympathetic valuation of other ways of life than our own. Malinowski has gone so far as to write of "the respect due even to savages." [9] And Herskovits states the positive element in the doctrine very clearly. He is not confused into supposing that cultural relativism is a mere scientific method, a procedure instrumental in reaching statements as to fact. No, he says, "cultural relativism is a *philosophy* which, in recognizing the values set up by every society to guide its own life, lays stress on the dignity inherent in every body of custom, and on the need for tolerance of conventions though they may differ from one's own." [10] And again: "Emphasis on the worth of many ways of life, not one, is an affirmation of the values of each culture." [11]

However, the two parts of this doctrine are not logically

or necessarily interdependent. The first part says that people are brought up to see the value in things that their local experience has suggested. The second part says that we should respect all cultures. But there is no true "therefore" between these two parts. It cannot be proved, from the proposition that values are relative, that we ought to respect all systems of values. We might just as well hate them all. (This point has been made by H. G. Barnett [12] and by David Bidney.[13]) It is Professor Herskovits who has intruded upon the objectivity of science a moral judgment, which I personally admire, but for which he can show no demonstration of proof.

The anthropologist is, then, ethically neutral, but unlike him of whom the partisan demanded, "Just who are you neutral *for?*", the anthropologist is neutral for everybody. This, at least, is the way anthropologists represent their position. It seems to me that their success in living up to their doctrine may be questioned.

The difficulties of doing so were remarked by not a few of the anthropologists themselves when in 1947 the Executive Board of their American professional association submitted a statement to the Commission on Human Rights of the United Nations. The statement urged the Commission to recognize that, not only should the personality of the individual be accorded respect, but that "respect for the cultures of differing human groups is equally important." [14] It declared the principle of cultural relativity and told the UN Commission that therefore any attempt it might make to write something about human rights ("formulate postulates") "that grow out of the beliefs or moral codes of one culture must to that extent detract from the applicability of any declaration of Human Rights to mankind as a whole." [15] So the Commission was advised to incorporate in the Declaration of Human Rights a statement of the right of men to live in terms of their own traditions.

I understand that the UN Commission did not follow this advice. I imagine that some anthropologists are rather relieved that they did not. Such a declaration might seem to authorize the head-hunting peoples to continue head hunting, for would they not, by continuing head hunting, be living in terms of their own traditions? Of course the anthropologists who drafted this statement were not thinking of the head hunters. They knew, as well as you or I, that the head hunters and the cannibals will not be permitted to live in terms of these particular traditions if it is our heads and bodies they go for. They were thinking of the great and influential world civilizations—Indonesian, Indian, Chinese, African, Euro-American. But even here it is not clear just what the writers of the declaration expected to guarantee to these traditional ways of life—the right of a Mississippi human group to maintain its traditional white supremacy, of Russia to maintain a dehumanizing, fear-ridden way of life? At the time the anthropologists wrote their statement it was perhaps nazism that presented to their minds most plainly the difficulties with their statement, for they wrote in the following sentence: "Even where political systems exist that deny citizens the right of participation in their government, or seek to conquer weaker peoples, underlying cultural values may be called on to bring the peoples of such states to a realization of the consequences of the acts of their governments." [16] If we call upon underlying values to save us, it is we, on the outside of the culture, who are making them effective. And what if the underlying approved values are not there? The sentence is, to put it bluntly, a weasel; by including it, the declaration was made self-contradictory. You either respect all values or you do not. If the Nazis had come to have values approving the subjugation of everybody else, we, or the United Nations, would have either to respect this traditional way of life or not respect it. Both Julian Steward and H. G. Barnett, anthropologists, saw that this follows, and agreed that anthropology cannot say anything as to whether one way of life is better than another.[17]

Perhaps they cannot. But their position while they say nothing is difficult. Among the anthropological commentators on the declaration about which I have been talking, there was much difference of judgment as to how to behave in their difficulty. One [18] would have them say nothing as to the good or bad in cultures. Another [19] would have them express such value judgments, but explicitly as moralists, not as anthropologists. A third pointed out that, as anthropologists are actors in society, they affect what is done to or about cultures by saying something or by saying nothing as to values, and so, being in fact unfree to abstain, should speak their valuations in order to realize their ends as citizens.[20]

The professed ethical neutrality of anthropology is not so uncomfortably challenged when it is an isolated primitive society at which the anthropologist is looking. It is not challenged, but it seems to slip a little—in favor of the stable and well integrated society. As one writer, not an anthropologist, put it: "Indignation is felt when the monograph records that the rhythm of the old dances is now beaten out on a biscuit tin instead of a drum." [21] I am sure that I have lamented the decline in folk arts in Mexico or in China. This tendency to betray some preference for the old ways in an exotic society is, I suppose, stimulated by the fact that the comparison of cultures, as unchanging systems, has been a principal task of anthropology until more recent times, when acculturation and the troubles of the personality have become matters for anthropologists to study. It is perhaps also induced by the attractiveness of a system of ideas that natives find convincing and satisfying and that anthropologists find logically coherent.

As soon as the anthropologist puts his attention on the particular human individuals in a primitive society, it becomes difficult to avoid the suggestion if not the fact that he is valuing one culture, or cultural situation, as better than another. It is not uncommon for an anthropologist, now studying a primitive culture disorganized by its contact with civilization, to see that the people he is studying are less comfortable than they were. Some of them, indeed, as those Oceanic natives whom Rivers described, appear now on their way to extinction just because they do not find life worth living any more. The anthropologist can hardly convince us—or himself—that so far as he is concerned a disorganized culture that fails to provide a desire to live is as valid as any other. Equal validity can be safely attributed only to cultures that arrange it so people do what they want to do and are convinced that it is the right thing to do.

But even among such cultures, the well-integrated and the motive-providing, it is not always possible for the anthropologist to avoid at least the suggestion that he is preferring one of them to another. Ruth Benedict was a cultural relativist who told us that cultures are equally valid. Nevertheless, in reading some of her pages, one doubts that she found them equally good. In the seventh chapter of *Patterns of Culture* she introduces the concept of "social waste." Here she leads the reader to see a resemblance between the values of Kwakiutl society and those of his own (Middletown); both emphasize rivalry. But rivalry, wrote

Benedict, is "notoriously wasteful. It ranks low in the scale of human values." One asks, Whose scale? Is there a universal scale of values which ranks rivalry low? She goes on to point out not only that "Kwakiutl rivalry produces a waste of material goods," but also that "the social waste is obvious." In Middletown, also, rivalry is "obsessive." Thus she is led to the conclusion that "it is possible to scrutinize different institutions and cast up their cost in terms of social capital, in terms of the less desirable behavior traits they stimulate, and in terms of human suffering and frustration." Apparently "social waste" includes a poor choice of desired behavior traits, human suffering, and frustration. In this passage [22] Benedict is saying how, within one society (that of Middletown) one might make an evaluation, a sort of scoring, of the social waste that follows from one set of institutions rather than another.

Is she here simply saying: You people in Middletown have chosen not to be frustrated, not to suffer, and not to be always at each other's throats; therefore, cast up the account of the success of your institutions in realizing these ends, and see if they are adapted to these ends? Is she leaving Middletown to choose to be frustrated if it pleases? I doubt it. She did not hesitate to say of the Kwakiutl that their rivalry produced an obvious social waste. If one knows what social waste is, why is it not possible to compare and evaluate, as to the amount of social waste produced, the cultures of Dobu and Zuni, or of Middletown and Bali? The line between description and evaluation is here unclear. It is very hard to say that culture A produces more suffering and frustration than does culture B without saying also that in this respect you prefer culture B.

It is that disturbing fellow, the living human individual,

who makes trouble for the scientist's stern principle of perfect objectivity. Whenever the anthropologist looks at him, something human inside the anthropologist stirs and responds. It is easy enough to be objective toward objects; but the human individual refuses to be only an object. When he is there before you, he insists on being judged as human beings are judged in life, if not in science. While the anthropologist is looking at the bones of the dead, at flint implements, or at institutions formally conceived and named—the Omaha kinship system or the tribal ideology —he is not much distracted by these claims upon his own human nature. But when the anthropologist meets and talks with some particular Indian or Oceanic islander, then he is apt to feel for that native while he is trying to describe him objectively. If the society is one that is running along the traditional ways of life, the field ethnologist is apt to respond with sympathy and indeed with favor toward the culture that keeps men's lives going in directions that they find good. If the ethnologist is himself gifted in communicating the human warmth of an exotic scene, as was Malinowski, an account results which communicates not only the humanity of the life described, but something of the enjoyment and satisfactions which the ethnologist himself experienced in coming to know that life. If the culture is one which puts the people who live by it into constant and fearful anxieties, the anthropologist is apt to show the disfavor he feels toward such a life. Reo Fortune's Dobuans are familiar; so I mention here instead the Tzeltal Indians of Chiapas, where Alfonso Villa Rojas found a people often sick, always believing that each sickness was the result of some moral transgression committed by the sufferer or, more terribly, by some one of his near kinsmen, and who are continually ridden by anxiety and compulsions to con-

fess sins.[23] Villa has described this people objectively, in the sense that his report is well documented and obviously trustworthy. But it would be untrue to assert that he has not shown, strongly in conversation and of course much more reservedly in his written description, his own unfavorable view of such a life. Furthermore, if one reads such an account of a people whose traditional ways of life have been disrupted, as, for example, McGregor's account of a reservation community of Sioux Indians,[24] one finds oneself making value judgments that seem to reflect those of the writer, as to the somewhat unhappy predicament in which these people find themselves.

I think that the objectivity claimed by the anthropologist must admit of difficulties and qualifications. Professor Herskovits declares that "a basic necessity of ethnographic research . . . calls for a rigid exclusion of value judgments." [25] This seems a little too strongly put. Rather, I should say, ethnographic research calls for as much objectivity as can be combined with the necessity to come to know the values of the people one is studying. The exception to allow the ethnographer to respect—i.e., value positively—all cultures, has already been noted. Professor R. H. Tawney is then expressing an opinion with which we may suppose that Professor Herskovits would agree when he writes that the student of a society must bring to his study "respect and affection." [26] The necessity to understand the values of the people one is studying requires, I should say, the projection into unfamiliar words and action of human qualities—sympathy, pride, wish to be appreciated, and so on. Otherwise the ethnologist will not find out what the people he is studying are proud about or what, for them, deserves appreciation. My own opinion is that it is not possible to make use of these human qual-

ities in field work, as I think one must, without also valuing
what one sees. In the very necessity to describe the n⸱
one must feel for him—or perhaps against him. The feel-
ings are mixed with valuations. In Indian communities in
which I have worked, I have found myself constantly lik-
ing and disliking some people as compared with others,
some customs as compared with others, and some aspects
of the total culture as compared with others. I remember,
after having spent a good deal of time in Chan Kom, Yucatan, how I had come to admire a certain quality of decency
and dignity about the people, and how bored I had become
with their—to me—overemphasis on the prudent and the
practical. If they would only once admire a sunset or report
a mystic experience, I used to hear myself thinking. I would
not know how to find out about a culture without this sort
of valuing. Objectivity requires that I hold in suspense
each formulation I make about the native life. It requires
me to become aware of the values I have that may lead me
in one direction rather than another. It demands that I
subject my descriptions to the tests of documentation, internal consistency, and if possible the evidence and judgments of other observers. But I do not think that it asks of
me that I divest myself of the human qualities, including
valuing. I could not do my work without them.[27]

It is not quite realistic to conceive of the ethnologist's
objectivity as excluding all valuing, or as permitting only
universal benevolence toward all cultures. We must get
along with something less rigid, less pure, than that.
Rather, field ethnology is an unsolvable paradox, a management of inconsistencies. In the words of J. C. Furnas, no
anthropologist but a man wise about anthropologists, "The
ethnologist must arrive at subjective sympathy with his
material while maintaining an extracultural objectivity that

is obviously impossible this side of sanity." [28] Furnas thinks that for someone who can really manage this paradox we shall have to wait for the Man from Mars, as Montaigne is dead.

If valuing is a part of the ethnologist's work, and if, as we know, ethnologists like other people differ as to the values they place on things, we shall have accounts of cultures that differ in part because of the differing values of the ethnologists. Or is it true that it makes no difference what are the ethnologist's values, that any set is as good as another in his toolbox? Apparently Dr. Oscar Lewis shared my view that the ethnologist cannot help using some of his values in his field work, for when he took me kindly to task in connection with my early description of the Mexican village of Tepoztlán, he made no objection to the fact that I had values when I studied the community. [29] His criticism (among others) was to the particular value system he felt he saw in my work. Apparently I had the wrong one. I think Dr. Lewis finds too much when he says my values there "contain the old Rousseauan notion of primitive peoples as noble savages," nor do I think that if he looks again he will find in my writings expression "of the corollary that with civilization has come the fall of man." [30] Perhaps he would be glad merely to accept my confession that I saw and suggested to the reader of my book certain good things in Tepoztlán: a sense of conviction in the people as to what life is all about; and a richness of the expressive life of the community. The general question, of which my own case is of course only an illustration, is whether this kind of positive value on certain aspects of native life is unfortunate for the work that results.

It is hard, I think, to make sure that failures to report certain aspects of native life are due to the particular choice of values. My own failures of the sort in Tepoztlán may have been due to inexperience, or to the lack of development of anthropological science, or to my personal incapacities. If the positive values I held did influence my work toward ignoring the unhappiness and anxiety about practical problems that I suppose existed in Tepoztlán, perhaps, on the other hand, the presence of those values in myself helped to bring out aspects of the life consistent with them. Dr. Lewis, in his work done much later in the same community, brought his own values to the field, for he is at least willing in his book to imagine himself as providing information and suggestions to "administrators, social scientists and others concerned with the problem of improving life in communities like Tepoztlán." Improvement would then consist of trying to make agriculture produce more and in substituting scientific understanding for "superstition and primitive beliefs." [31] The ethnologist who brings to the field the value judgment that science and modern technology are superior to magic and primitive technology I should think would be particularly interested in problems of production. And if he is interested in—and so places values on—personal adjustments between people, he will, I think, tell us things that help us to understand the personal adjustments or maladjustments of the people he is describing. Perhaps we should ask of the field ethnologist, not that he divest himself of values, for that is impossible, nor that he emphasize in every case values predominating in his own times with regard to applied science, increased production, and adjusted personalities, but that he make plain what he does find that is good or bad about the people he reports. And then, also, perhaps he can help to bring it about that he is followed in the same community to be studied by an ethnologist with a contrasting value emphasis! It was the *New Yorker* that suggested that we do not want balanced textbooks; we want balanced libraries. We do not want ethnologists so balanced that they have no humanity. We want a balanced profession, a varied lot of anthropologists.

In this chapter I have so far said that anthropologists, confronting this or that primitive society, do in fact place values of their own on what they see there, although they often say that they do not. Also, I have said that in my opinion their practice is better than their preaching, for I think that this valuing, guarded by all the objectivity and scientific procedure they can muster, is a necessary part of their work. So far I have had in mind the ordinary ethnological confrontation in which one ethnologist looks at one or a few contemporary primitive societies, as they exist, now, without giving thought to the human biography. Now I take up this question as to whether anthropologists do value what they see in their studies of the whole of human history. I am now thinking of the value judgments that may be placed on primitive cultures in the light of the transition from precivilized living to civilization. I am asking whether anthropologists judge a primitive culture by the same standards by which they judge Russia or the United States. I am entertaining the possibility that there is some consistency of the valuation of cultures that does go on, both by laymen and by anthropologists, and that this consistency is shaped by historical fact: a transformation that has come about in ethical judgment. I am, perhaps, extending somewhat the doctrine of cultural relativity: I am saying that the standards of truth and goodness are relative to a great historic cultural difference, that between uncivilized people and civilized people.

These ideas have been in part suggested to me by something written by J. C. Furnas, whom I have already quoted in this chapter. In his book, *The Anatomy of Paradise*, occur the following six sentences:

It is disquietingly true that, as Boas pointed out, "primitive society . . . does not favor individual freedom of thought,"—a generality hardly worth making if a generic difference had not been felt between the world of *tabu* without formal law and the world that at least wrote, however imperfectly it observes, bills of rights. Or take it this way: For generations the western world has bitterly blamed western man for the crime of not understanding the savage. It seems never to occur to anybody that, other things being equal, it would be equally fair to blame the savage for not understanding western man. Since that would obviously be absurd, the two sets of cultures are unmistakably on different levels, a statement that can be made without specifying higher and lower. Western man has something which neither the preliterate nor any of his ancestors possess or ever did possess, something that imposes the privilege and complicating duty of intellectual integrity, self-criticism, and generalized disinterestedness. If there is such a thing as the white man's burden, this is it.[32]

The anthropologist impliedly recognizes a total trend of history which has given him an instrument for reaching truth that he regards as inherently better—not just better relative to the judgment impressed on him by his enculturated experience. What the anthropologist says about the magic practiced in a primitive society is to the anthropologist really truer, in some sense, than what the native says about it. Dr. Lewis suggests that the Tepoztecans would be better off with less magic and more applied science. I do not think that he feels he is expressing merely an enculturated judgment no more valid than what a preliterate native would say on the subject. When Dr. Hersko-

vits tells us that, with the possible exception of technological aspects, the proposition that one way of thought is
better than another is exceedingly difficult to establish, he
does not mean that this statement is valid only for his own
culture, but he means it universally and would claim that
it holds true for all people, although only those will accept
it who are capable of understanding what is intended by
it.[33] Anthropologists, like other people around them, recognize a double standard of excellence in finding the truth.
The primitive man is not expected to reach the kind of
truth we call scientific with the same success with which
civilized man is expected to reach it. There has been a
transformation of judgment as to truth.

But I say also that there has been a transformation as
to judgment as to the good. The moral order has been provided with measures of excellence unknown and unknow-
able in precivilized society. The anthropologist, insofar as
his describing involves, as I think it does, some valuing,
makes use of these new measures, and does not expect his
subject matter, the preliterate people, to make use of them
in valuing him.

When the anthropologists helped modern people to see
that the nineteenth-century belief in progress was a faith,
not a proven fact, they threw out the baby with the bath
so far that its persisting cry to be heard could not reach
their ears. One kind of total trend of history they did admit,
the accumulation of technology, as well as the related
development of science.[34] But they have on the whole followed Boas, who wrote in 1930 that "it is much more difficult to speak of progress in any cultural activity" and
that fundamental ethical attitudes have shown a "lack of
change." [35] This is saying that progress, in the sense of a

described fact of historical change, is limited to the development of technology.

Writing fifteen or more years later, Kroeber looked again at the questions as to whether history showed man's progress and found more than Boas had found. Kroeber states "three approaches that seem to yield at least a partial standard of what constitutes 'higher' or more advanced culture, apart from mere quantity of it." [36] One of these three is the cumulative development of technology and science. The other two standards for judging a culture as "higher" or "more advanced," according to Kroeber, lead us into recognition of differences between precivilized and civilized peoples with regard to, respectively, the true and the good.

"The first is the criterion of magic and 'superstition.'" By this Kroeber means that people who have visions or other experiences that in modern society are regarded as neurotic or psychotic are in preliterate societies highly valued, along with the experiences. "Retarded peoples," he writes, "invert the emphasis. . . . To them a child or a hawk or a stone seen or heard in a certain kind of dream or trance is much more important than a physical child or hawk or stone that one can touch and handle, because it is the possible source of much more power." [37] Therefore he concludes, "The bestowal of social rewards for the inability to distinguish subjective experiences from objective phenomena, or for the deliberate inversion of the two, is a presumable mark of lack of progress." [38] In these passages Kroeber recognizes a transformation in judgment as to the truth as precivilized living gave way to civilization. The principle of cultural relativism leads the anthropologist to look sympathetically at the view that primitive man takes of these experiences when the anthropologist is attentive to the moral and religious values that are, for the primitive person, involved in these mistakes of judgment as to the truth. On the other hand, when the visions and magical beliefs lead to sickness or cruelty, the anthropologist, who is then apt to think that scientific knowledge is better than magical mistakes, will pass an unfavorable value judgment on such primitive customs, and perhaps help the administrator to reduce the sickness or end the cruelty.

The other criterion for progress which Kroeber finds is even more interesting. He describes this great trend in history as the "decline of infantile obsession with the outstanding physiological events of human life." [39] The primitive person allows to obtrude into public recognition and the social order "blood and death and decay." Kroeber's long list of primitive customs which exhibit this obtrusion evokes these, to us, disagreeable facts; I do not quote the list here; it includes blood sacrifice, wearing of skull or jaws by widows, ritual prostitution, and cannibalism. Kroeber reminds us that such practices are not uniformly present in preliterate societies; rather we have here "a probable tendency that holds good on the whole or in the long run." [40]

Now in recognizing this great trend in human history, Kroeber is speaking of the entire human race in its historic movement toward civilization. This trend is more or less true for people everywhere. In China, as in the West, blood sacrifice gave way to symbolic offerings. All the world religions, he says, set their influence "on the prohumane and anti-infantile side." [41]

Second, it needs to be emphasized that Kroeber has identified here a change in human valuing. He is not simply saying that certain customs, which one might, from the outside, describe objectively, have become less common or have disappeared. He is saying that men, on the whole, have come to assume a different standard for judging, in these respects, what is good and bad. He says: "Cultures which have once abandoned such practices react with aversion, disgust, revulsion, or the shame of bad taste." [42] Moreover, while Kroeber begins his discussion of this change in valuing with the change in the attitude taken toward the obtrusion of physiological facts, as he develops his idea he begins to extend the scope of this change in valuing so that something more than disgust with public obtrusion of blood and corpses is meant. He says that as men become more civilized they are less concerned "with the gratifications of the ego." Advanced cultures exhibit "concern about humaneness. The latter is manifest also in trends like those of opposition to slavery, torture as a judicial procedure, beatings as legal punishment, execution with torture, slaughter of prisoners of war." [43] I do not think that the recent return of some of these things in civilized society would require Kroeber to alter what he has written as to an over-all trend of history. By his words we are reminded that along with the growing disgust with blood and decay and violence toward the human body goes a growing concern for the welfare and dignity of others. Humaneness is bigger and wider than personal fastidiousness. Kroeber is recognizing a transformation in ethical judgment.

If we follow Kroeber, we shall not hesitate to accept the words of Furnas that I have already quoted: "The two sets of cultures (precivilized and civilized) are unmistakably on different levels." The insistence of many anthropologists that all cultures are equivalent allows some qualification. Kroeber, in spite of the refusal of anthropologists to say anything that might sound as if primitive people were earlier than or figuratively ancestral to civilized men,[44] does not hesitate to call the precivilized societies "infantile" and the civilized societies "more adult." The standards as to the good have changed with history. The moral canon tends to mature. The change is far from steady, and the future course of the ethical judgment is not, it seems to me, assured to us. But in this sense—that on the whole the human race has come to develop a more decent and humane measure of goodness—there has been a transformation of ethical judgment which makes us look at noncivilized peoples, not as equals, but as people on a different level of human experience.

I find it impossible to regret that the human race has tended to grow up. As in the maturing of the individual, there are losses and gains. There are, especially, new responsibilities. The responsibility to look at the cultures of other peoples in the light of civilized ethical judgment is one of these. I think we do in fact appraise the conduct of primitive people by standards different from those by which we judge civilized people and yet also—and this is harder to say convincingly—according to the historic trend which has tended to make the totality of human conduct more decent and more humane. We do not expect the preliterate person to cultivate and protect individual freedom of thought as we expect civilized people to do. We do not blame the Veddah for failing to have a subtle graphic art. We understand how it is that the Siriono husband leaves his wife to die alone in the jungle, and we do not condemn him as we condemn the suburban husband who leaves his wife to die in a snowdrift. We do not expect a people to have a moral norm that their material conditions of life make impossible. On the other hand, when a people surmount the difficulties of their material conditions to reach a moral norm which puts them, by so much, on the road which civilization has taken, we value highly what they do. I praise the Yagua for respecting privacy under conditions of living that make privacy difficult to respect.

We judge the conduct of primitive peoples—as of other people—by their success in acting in accordance with the ideals they have chosen. When my Yucatecan Maya friends caught a wild animal, doused it in gasolene, and set fire to it, I condemned the act strongly, partly for the reason that they have set up ideals of kindliness and compassion to animals too. They have plainly gone wrong. There is an aspect of their act which is more to be condemned than the torture of prisoners by the Huron. At least I can see that torture, which I also condemn, bears some relation, among the Huron, to ideals of fortitude and courage.

For we also judge the conduct of a primitive people by the degree to which the ideals they have chosen conform to the conceptions that have developed in history as to what human beings ought to be. These conceptions, as I have tried to suggest in this essay, are in part local, in part more or less universal. I cannot prove to you that man should act more decently and more humanely. I follow Kroeber in saying that on the whole he has come to. When, now, he does not, it is a worse mistake than when he did not in pre-civilized times. We have come to know better, however "better" is to be justified philosophically. I say only that these changing conceptions are drawn from or confirmed by history. Thus I can see some good in Huron customs while I abominate the torture.

My praise of Petalesharoo here receives explanation, if not justification. Petalesharoo acted against the customary practice of his people. It is a little easier to do that after civilization than before; in precivilized societies it was harder. So Petalesharoo gets my praise on that count. And when he acted, he acted in conformity with the trend of the human career of which he was ignorant, but which I know about, being some thousands of years older in civilization than was he. So it is not remarkable that I praise him. Perhaps also you, my reader, do too.

If you do, and you are not an anthropologist, no one will scold. But I am an anthropologist, and have taken the oath of objectivity. Somehow the broken pledge—if it is broken —sits lightly on my conscience. In me, man and anthropologist do not separate themselves sharply. I used to think I could bring about that separation in scientific work about humanity. Now I have come to confess that I have not effected it, and indeed to think that it is not possible to do so. All the rules of objectivity I should maintain: the marshaling of evidence that may be confirmed by others, the persistent doubting and testing of all important descriptive formulations that I make, the humility before the facts, and the willingness to confess oneself wrong and begin over. I hope I may always strive to obey these rules. But I think now that what I see men do, and understand as something that human beings do, is seen often with a valuing of it. I like or dislike as I go. This is how I reach understanding of it. The double standard of ethical judgment toward primitive peoples is a part of my version of cultural relativity. It is because I am a product of civilization that I value as I do. It is because I am a product of civilization that I have both a range of experience within which to do my understanding-valuing and the scientific disciplines that help me to describe what I value so that others will accept it, or, recognizing it as not near enough the truth, to correct it. And if, in this too I am wrong, those others will correct me here also.

Notes

The publishers of the following books and journals kindly gave permission to quote certain passages: the lines on pp. 12–13 from "The Folk Society," by Robert Redfield, *American Journal of Sociology,* LII (January, 1947), University of Chicago Press; lines on p. 175 from B. Malinowki's "Magic, Science and Religion," in *Science, Religion and Reality,* edited by Joseph Needham, The Macmillan Co., 1925; and the lines on p. 158 from *Anatomy of Paradise,* by J. C. Furnas, William Sloan Associates, Inc., 1948.

INTRODUCTION

1. V. Gordon Childe, *New Light on the Most Ancient East* (London: K. Paul, Trench, Trubner & Co., 1935); *Man Makes Himself* (2nd ed.; London: Watts and Co., 1941, first published 1936); *What Happened in History* (Harmondsworth, Middlesex: Penguin Books, 1942); *Social Evolution* (London: Watts and Co., 1951).

2. Robert J. Braidwood, *The Near East and the Foundations for Civilization* (Condon Lectures, Oregon State System of Higher Education, Eugene, Ore., 1952).

3. For a characterization of folk society by an anthropologist, see A. L. Kroeber, *Anthropology* (New York: Harcourt, Brace and Co., 1948), pp. 280–286. See also Ralph Linton, *The Study of Man* (New York and London: D. Appleton-Century Co., 1936), pp. 283–284.

4. Howard Becker, *Ionia and Athens: Studies in Secularization* (Ph.D. dissertation, University of Chicago, 1930); Becker, "Sacred and Secular Societies," *Social Forces,* XXVIII (May, 1950), 361–376; Howard W. Odum, *Understanding Society: The Principles of Dynamic Sociology* (New York: Macmillan Co., 1947), p. 260; Robert Redfield, "The Folk Society," *American Journal of Sociology,*

LII (January 1947), 293–308; Horace Miner, "The Folk-Urban Continuum, *American Sociological Review,* XVII (October, 1952), 529–537; Gideon Sjoberg, "Folk and 'Feudal' Societies," *American Journal of Sociology,* LVIII (November, 1952), 231–239.

CHAPTER I

1. Melville Herskovits, *Man and His Works* (New York: A. A. Knopf, 1948), p. 71.

2. Sol Tax, "Revolution and the Process of Civilization," *Human Origins, An Introductory General Course in Anthropology, Selected Readings,* Series II (2nd ed.; Chicago: University of Chicago Press, 1946, mimeographed).

3. Gutorm Gjessing, *Norges Steinalder* (Oslo: Taslum, 1945).

4. V. Gordon Childe, *Prehistoric Migrations in Europe* (Oslo: Aschehoug; Cambridge, Harvard University Press, 1950), p. 6.

5. *Ibid.,* pp. 5–6.

6. *Ibid.,* p. 11.

7. Childe, *What Happened in History* (Harmondsworth, Middlesex: Penguin Books, 1942), p. 53; *Man Makes Himself* (2nd ed.; London: Watts and Co., 1941, first published in 1936), pp. 86–87.

8. George C. Homans, *English Villagers of the Thirteenth Century* (Cambridge: Harvard University Press, 1941).

9. Childe, *Prehistoric Migrations,* p. 7.

10. *Ibid.*

11. Childe, *Social Evolution* (London: Watts and Co., 1951).

12. A. R. Radcliffe-Brown, "Three Tribes of Western Australia," *Journal of the Royal Anthropological Institute,* XLIII (1913), 150–151.

13. Childe, *Prehistoric Migrations,* p. 7.

14. Karl Polanyi, *The Great Transformation* (New York and Toronto: Farrar & Rinehart, 1944).

15. Polanyi, "Our Obsolete Market Mentality," *Commentary,* III (February, 1947), 112.

16. Childe, *Prehistoric Migrations,* p. 16.

17. Robert Redfield, "The Folk Society," *American Journal of Sociology,* LII (January, 1947), 299.

18. Herbert Blumer, "Moulding of Mass Behavior through the Motion Picture," *Publications of the American Sociological Society,* XXIX (August, 1935), 115–127.

19. A. L. Kroeber, *Anthropology* (New York: Harcourt, Brace and Co., 1948), p. 282.

20. Redfield, *op. cit.*, p. 300.

21. Bronislaw Malinowski, *Magic, Science and Religion* (Boston: Beacon Press, 1948).

22. Ruth Bunzel, *The Pueblo Potter, A Study of Creative Imagination in Primitive Art* (Ph.D. dissertation, Columbia University, 1929), p. 52.

23. Childe, *Prehistoric Migrations*, p. 7.

24. Childe, *What Happened in History*, p. 35.

25. Charles P. Mountford, *Brown Men and Red Sand* (Melbourne: Robertson and Mullens, 1948).

26. Eliseo Vivas, *The Moral Life and the Ethical Life* (Chicago: University of Chicago Press, 1950), p. 105.

27. Allen R. Holmberg, *Nomads of the Long Bow, the Siriono of Eastern Bolivia,* Smithsonian Institution, Institute of Social Anthropology, Pub. No. 10 (Washington, 1950).

28. Paul Fejos, *Ethnography of the Yagua* (New York: Viking Fund, 1943).

29. C. H. Cooley, *Social Organization* (New York, C. Scribner's Sons, 1909), p. 54.

30. Robert Ezra Park, *Human Communities* (Glencoe, Ill.: Free Press, 1952), pp. 22–32, 35.

31. *Ibid.*, p. 24.

32. Clyde Kluckhohn and others, "Values and Value-Orientation," *The Theory of Social Action,* ed. by Parsons and Shils (Cambridge: Harvard University Press, 1951).

33. Childe, "The Urban Revolution," *Town Planning Review,* XXI (1950), 3–17. Childe says that these ten criteria are "all deducible from archaeological data." He must include in such data written records, for several of these criteria are made known to us only through written records. And this fact reminds us of the possibility that certain of these criteria of civilization—accumulation of capital, writing (insofar as begun on perishable materials), the beginnings of science, full-time specialists possibly, and a privileged ruling class—might have had their beginnings in the life of those Middle Eastern towns that preceded the building of the first true cities.

CHAPTER II

1. Arnold J. Toynbee, *A Study of History,* abridgement of Volumes I–VI by D. C. Somervell (New York and London: Oxford University Press, 1947), p. 49.

2. Karl A. Wittfogel, "Die Theorie der orientalischen Gesellschaft," *Zeitschrift für Sozialforschung*, VII (1938), 90–122.

3. Toynbee, *op. cit.*, p. 414.

4. A. L. Kroeber, *Anthropology* (rev. ed.; New York: Harcourt Brace and Co., 1948), pp. 418–425.

5. V. Gordon Childe, *What Happened in History* (Harmondsworth, Middlesex: Penguin Books, 1942), p. 133.

6. Raymond Firth, *Malay Fishermen: Their Peasant Economy* (London: Kegan Paul, Trench, Trubner & Co., 1946), pp. 22–27.

7. Hsiao-Tung Fei, *Peasant Life in China* (New York: E. P. Dutton & Co., 1939), p. 267.

8. *Ibid.*

9. John F. Embree, *Suye Mura, A Japanese Village* (Chicago: University of Chicago Press, 1939), pp. 138–153.

10. McKim Marriott, personal communication, "In the far south, and especially on the Malabar side."

11. A. S. Altekar, *A History of Village Communities in Western India* (Bombay: Oxford University Press, 1929), p. 11.

12. Fei, *op. cit.*, pp. 274–280.

13. Henry S. Maine, *Village-Communities in the East and West* (3rd ed.; London: John Murray, 1907).

14. McKim Marriott, personal communication.

15. *Ibid.* However, as to the present situation in villages of India, Marriott adds that the largest part of the villagers' credit is provided by landlord, shopkeepers, or well-to-do peasants of the peasant's own or neighboring community.

16. A. R. Radcliffe-Brown, "Three Tribes of Western Australia," *Journal of the Royal Anthropological Institute,* XLIII (1913), 150–151.

17. Altekar, *op. cit.*, p. 114.

18. Arthur H. Smith, *Village Life in China* (New York: Fleming H. Revell Co., 1899), pp. 54–69.

19. Childe, *What Happened in History,* p. 111.

20. Alfonso Villa Rojas, *The Maya of East Central Quintana Roo* (Washington: Carnegie Institution of Washington, 1945), pp. 48, 161 ff.

21. Robert Redfield and Alfonso Villa Rojas, *Chan Kom, A Maya Village* (Washington: Carnegie Institution of Washington, 1934).

22. P. Sorokin and C. Zimmerman, *Principles of Rural-Urban Sociology* (New York: H. Holt & Co., 1929), p. 332.

23. E. K. L. Francis, "The Personality Type of the Peasant according to Hesiod's *Works and Days*," *Rural Sociology*, X (September, 1945), 275–295.

24. W. I. Thomas and Florian Znaniecki, *The Polish Peasant in Europe and America* (1st ed.; Boston: Richard C. Badger, 1918–1920; 2nd ed.; New York: Alfred A. Knopf, 1927).

25. W. Reymont, *The Peasants* (New York: Alfred A. Knopf, 1925).

26. Christopher Dawson, *The Age of the Gods* (London: Sheed & Ward, 1933).

27. Kroeber, *op. cit.*, p. 284.

28. Henri Troyat, *Pushkin, A Biography*, tr. by Randolph T. Weaver (New York: Pantheon, 1950), p. 13.

29. *Time, Space and Man*, prepared by the Department of Anthropology of the University of Chicago under the direction of R. J. Braidwood, W. M. Krogman, and Sol Tax (Chicago: University of Chicago Press, 1946). (A new edition is in preparation under the direction of R. J. Braidwood, Sol Tax, and S. L. Washburn.)

30. Childe, *What Happened in History*, p. 123.

31. *Ibid.*, p. 126 ff.

32. Toynbee, *op. cit.*, p. 394 ff.

33. *Ibid.*, p. 394.

34. Robert E. Park, *Race and Culture* (Glencoe, Ill.: Free Press, 1950), pp. 345–392.

35. See the career of Don Eustaquio Ceme of Chan Kom, as recorded in Redfield and Villa, *Chan Kom,* and in Robert Redfield, *A Village that Chose Progress* (Chicago: University of Chicago Press, 1950). Don Eus, in his deliberate cultivation of the townsman's knowledge and in his reading of secular technical literature, led the intelligentsia of Chan Kom. Yet, in his continuing interest in and sympathy with the traditional sacred lore of his village, his attempts to reflect upon and systematize this lore, he belonged also to the literati. The circumstances under which the reconciliation can be made in a single personality might be investigated. The appearance of the literati in early Mesopotamian civilization is expressed in "school tablets" going back to the beginning of the third millennium B.C. See Samuel Noah Kramer, "The Sumerian School: A Pre-Greek System of Education," *Studies Presented to David Moore Robinson on his Seventieth Birthday*, ed. by G. E. Mylonas (St. Louis: Washington University, 1951), Vol. I.

36. Toynbee, *op. cit.*, p. 414.

37. J. H. Boeke, *The Evolution of the Netherlands East Indies*

Economy (New York: Netherlands and Netherlands Indies Council, Institute of Pacific Relations, 1946).

38. W. H. R. Rivers, ed., *Essays on the Depopulation of Melanesia* (Cambridge, Eng.: The University Press, 1922).

39. Melville J. Herskovits and Frances S. Herskovits, *Rebel Destiny among the Bush Negroes of Dutch Guiana* (New York and London: Whittlesey House, 1934).

40. Edward Spicer, *Pascua, A Yaqui Village in Arizona* (Chicago: University of Chicago Press, 1940).

41. Kroeber, *op. cit.*, p. 279.

42. Robert Redfield, *The Folk Culture of Yucatan* (Chicago: University of Chicago Press, 1941).

43. Childe, *What Happened in History,* p. 90.

44. Childe, *Man Makes Himself* (2nd ed.; London: Watts and Co., 1941), p. 171.

45. Toynbee, *op. cit.,* p. 375 ff.

46. *Ibid.,* p. 378.

47. *Ibid.,* p. 405.

48. *Ibid.,* p. 377.

49. Lionel Trilling, "Manners, Morals and the Novel," *The Liberal Imagination* (New York: Viking Press, 1950), pp. 206–207.

50. David Riesman, with the collaboration of Reuel Denney and Nathan Glazer, *The Lonely Crowd: A Study of the Changing American Character* (New Haven: Yale University Press, 1950).

CHAPTER III

1. Patrick Putnam, *The Pygmies of the Ituri Forest,* quoted in Carleton S. Coon, *A Reader in General Anthropology* (New York: Henry Holt and Co., 1948), p. 324.

2. Edward P. Dozier, "Resistance to Acculturation and Assimilation in an Indian Pueblo," *American Anthropologist,* LIII (January–March, 1951), 56–66.

3. *Amos* 3:6; 6:8.

4. Oswald Spengler, *The Decline of the West* (New York: Alfred A. Knopf, 1926), pp. 32–33.

5. *Ibid.,* p. 32.

6. Warde Fowler, *Religious Experience of the Roman People from the Earliest Times to the Age of Augustus* (London: Macmillan & Co., 1911); *Roman Festivals of the Period of the Republic: An Introduction to the Study of the Religion of the Romans* (London and New York: Macmillan & Co., 1899).

7. Cyril Bailey, *The Religion of Ancient Rome* (London: A. Constable & Co., 1907).

8. William Reginald Halliday, *Lectures on the History of Roman Religion from Numa to Augustus* (Boston: Small, Maynard & Co., 1927).

9. Robert Redfield and Alfonso Villa Rojas, *Chan Kom, A Maya Village* (Washington: Carnegie Institution of Washington, 1934).

10. Herbert J. Spinden, *Maya Dates and What They Reveal,* The Museum of the Brooklyn Institute of Arts and Sciences, Science Bulletin, IV (1930), 102.

11. Ralph L. Roys, *The Book of Chilam Balam of Chumayel* (Washington: Carnegie Institution of Washington, 1933).

12. *Ibid.,* p. 79.

13. Robert Redfield, *The Folk Culture of Yucatan* (Chicago: University of Chicago Press, 1941).

14. V. Gordon Childe, *What Happened in History* (2nd ed.; New York: Penguin Books, 1946; first published in 1942), p. 11.

15. A. N. Whitehead, *The Adventures of Ideas* (Harmondsworth, Middlesex: Penguin Books, 1948; first published in 1933), p. 27.

16. John A. Wilson, "Egypt," *The Intellectual Adventure of Ancient Man* by H. and H. A. Frankfort and others (Chicago: University of Chicago Press, 1946), p. 111.

17. Whitehead, *op. cit.,* p. 27.

CHAPTER IV

1. F. S. C. Northrop, *The Meeting of East and West* (New York: Macmillan Co., 1946).

2. Among many papers, see "The Relation of Habitual Thought and Behavior to Language," *Language, Culture, and Personality: Essays in Memory of Edward Sapir,* ed. by Leslie Spier and others (Menasha, Wis.: Sapir Memorial Publication Fund, 1941), pp. 75–93. An earlier view of the relations of language and world view appears in Fritz Graebner, *Das Weltbild der Primitiven* (Munich: Verlag Ernsst Reinhard, 1924), "IV. Weltanschauungen und Sprachen," pp. 72–94.

3. The "whole" of a way of life is still differently conceived and subdivided in Gregory Bateson's *Naven* (Cambridge, Eng.: the University Press, 1936) where "ethos" is used to mean the "culturally standardized system of organization of the instincts and emotions of the individuals," and "eidos" mean the cultural "standardization

NOTES TO CHAPTER IV

of the cognitive aspects of the personality of the individuals." So used, the terms refer to group character, or basic personality type, and "eidos" also relates to the forms and manner of thought characterizing the group.

4. Martin Heidegger, "The Age of the World View," *Measure,* II (Summer, 1951), 279.

5. See, for example, Clyde Kluckhohn, "The World View of the Navaho," *Ideological Foundations of World Order,* ed. by F. S. C. Northrop (New Haven: Yale University Press, 1949), pp. 356–384.

6. Paul Radin, *Primitive Man as Philosopher* (New York and London: D. Appleton & Co., 1927).

7. George Peter Murdock, "The Common Denominator of Cultures," *The Science of Man in the World Crisis,* ed. by Ralph Linton (New York: Columbia University Press, 1945), p. 124.

8. Quoted in George Devereux, "The Logical Foundations of Culture and Personality Studies," *Trans. of the New York Academy of Sciences,* Series II, VII (1945), 122.

9. Irving Hallowell, "The Self and Its Behavioral Environment," MS. To appear in *Psychoanalysis and the Social Sciences,* IV, ed. by Geza Roheim.

10. Margaret Mead, *Male and Female, A Study of the Sexes in a Changing World* (New York: William Morrow and Co., 1949).

11. Margaret Mead, "The Mountain Arapesh. II Supernaturalism," *Anthrop. Papers American Museum of Natural History,* XXXVII, pt. iii (New York, 1940), 319–451.

12. Ruth Bunzel, "Introduction to Zuni Ceremonialism, Zuni Origin Myths," etc., in *47th Annual Report of the Bureau of American Ethnology,* 1929–1930 (Washington, 1932), pp. 467 ff.

13. Thorkild Jacobsen, "Mesopotamia," *The Intellectual Adventure of Ancient Man* by H. and H. A. Frankfort and others (Chicago: University of Chicago Press, 1946), pp. 125–127.

14. Daniel J. Boorstin, *The Lost World of Thomas Jefferson* (New York: Henry Holt & Co., 1948).

15. A. N. Whitehead, *Adventures of Ideas* (Harmondsworth, Middlesex: Penguin Books, 1948; first published in 1933), p. 133.

16. Two other conceptions of the locus of order mentioned by Whitehead—law as description and law as conventional interpretation—are relevant to modern societies, with science, only.

17. Clyde Kluckhohn, "The Philosophy of the Navaho Indians," *Ideological Differences and World Order,* ed. by F. S. C. Northrop (New Haven: Yale University Press, 1949), p. 361.

18. V. Gordon Childe, *Social Evolution* (London: Watts and Co., 1951), p. 84.

19. H. and H. A. Frankfort, "Myth and Reality," *Intellectual Adventure of Ancient Man* (Chicago: University of Chicago Press, 1946), p. 4.

20. *Ibid.*, p. 6.

21. Dorothy D. Lee, *Religious Perspectives of College Teaching* (New Haven: Edward Hazen Foundation, no date), p. 7.

22. *Ibid.*, p. 6.

23. *Ibid.*, p. 13.

24. *Ibid.*, p. 6.

25. Jean Piaget, *The Moral Judgment of the Child* (London: K. Paul, Trench, Trubner & Co., 1932); Robert Havighurst, "Belief in Immanent Justice and Animism among Indian Children of the Southwest and Sioux," *MS,* Committee on Human Development, University of Chicago. Another interesting point brought out by this study was that Navaho children felt that the rules of *Indian* games were unchangeable; but that the rules of games introduced from the *whites* might be changed.

26. And as the leadership and power in society shifted from priests and priest-kings to merchants and other secular people, the disintegration of Man-Nature-God proceeded. "The whole story of the Renaissance shows within the limits of the city-state how the exhilarating rise of an urban civilization is liable to issue in a process of secularization—the priest as well as the noble loses the power that he was able to possess in a more conservative agrarian world. Something parallel has happened over and over again in the case of nation-states when not only have towns become really urban in character—which is late in the case of England, for example—but when a sort of leadership in society has passed to the towns . . ." (Herbert Butterfield, *Origins of Modern Science* [London: Bill, 1950], p. 67).

27. Jacobsen, *op. cit.,* p. 200.

28. H. and H. A. Frankfort, "The Emancipation of Thought from Myth," *The Intellectual Adventure of Ancient Man* (Chicago: University of Chicago Press, 1946), p. 377.

29. Sol Tax, "World View and Social Relations in Guatemala," *American Anthropologist,* n.s. XLIII (1944), 27–42. The Guatemalan case, described in this paper, indicates the possibilities of combining a primitive world view with impersonalized social relations. The Guatemalan Indians view nature as personal and concerned with man, yet the intersocietal relations are not unlike those

of a great city, and even within the local community there is a commercial spirit.

CHAPTER V

1. Weston La Barre, "The Age Period of Cultural Fixation," *Mental Hygiene,* XXXIII (New York: National Committee for Mental Hygiene, 1949), 221, 216–217.

2. G. B. Chisholm, "The Re-establishment of Peacetime Society," *The Psychiatry of Enduring Peace and Social Progress,* the William Alanson White Psychiatric Foundation (Washington, 1946).

3. Paul Radin, *Primitive Man as Philosopher* (New York and London: D. Appleton & Co., 1927).

4. "There is, of course, no widespread thirst for knowledge in a savage community, new things such as European topics bore them frankly and their whole interest is largely encompassed by the traditional world of their culture. But within this there is both the antiquarian mind passionately interested in myths, stories, details of customs, pedigrees and ancient happenings, and there is also to be found the naturalist, patient and painstaking in his observations, capable of generalization and of connecting long chains of events in the life of animals, and in the marine world or in the jungle. It is enough to realize how much European naturalists have often learned from their savage colleagues to appreciate this interest found in the native for nature. There is finally among the primitives, as every fieldworker well knows, the sociologist, the ideal informant capable with marvelous accuracy and insight to give the *raison d'etre,* the function, and the organization of many a simpler institution in his tribe." Bronislaw Malinowski, "Magic, Science and Religion," *Science, Religion and Reality,* ed. by Joseph Needham (New York: Macmillan Co., 1925), p. 36.

5. As summarized in *The Coming of the Maori* by Te Rangi Hiroa (Sir Peter Buck), (Wellington: Whitcombe and Tombs, 1950).

6. Marcel Griaule, *Dieu d'Eau, Entretiens avec Ogotemmeli* (Paris: Les editions du Chêne, no date).

7. Franz Boas, "Mythology and Folklore," *General Anthropology,* ed. by Franz Boas (New York: D. C. Heath and Co., 1938), p. 619.

8. H. and H. A. Frankfort and others, *The Intellectual Adventure of Ancient Man* (Chicago: University of Chicago Press, 1946).

9. *Ibid.,* pp. 55–61.

10. *Ibid.,* pp. 208–218.

11. George A. Pettitt, "Primitive Education in North America," *University of California Publications in American Archaeology and Ethnology*, XLIII (1946), 1–182; W. D. Hambly, *Origins of Education among Primitive Peoples* (London: Macmillan & Co., 1926); Claude Andrew Nichols, *Moral Education among the North American Indians* (New York: Bureau of Publications, Teachers College, Columbia University, 1930).

12. Margaret Mead, "Our Education Emphases in Primitive Perspective," *Education and the Cultural Process*, reprinted from the *American Journal of Sociology*, XLVIII (May, 1943), 9.

13. *Ibid.*, pp. 10–11. See also Margaret Mead, "Character Formation and Diachronic Theory," *Social Structure*, ed. by M. Fortes (Oxford: Clarendon Press, 1949).

14. Fred Eggan, *The Social Organization of the Western Pueblos* (Chicago: University of Chicago Press, 1950).

15. Camilla Wedgewood, "The Nature and Functions of Secret Societies," *Oceania*, I (1930), 129–145.

16. Reo Fortune, *Omaha Secret Societies* (New York: Columbia University Press, 1932).

17. Robert H. Lowie, *The Origin of the State* (New York: Harcourt, Brace and Co., 1927), pp. 94–111.

18. Karl Llewellyn and E. Adamson Hoebel, *The Cheyenne Way* (Norman: University of Oklahoma Press, 1941).

19. Ralph Linton, *The Study of Man* (New York and London: D. Appleton Co., 1936), p. 451.

20. Robert Lynd, *Middletown* (New York, Harcourt, Brace and Co., 1929).

21. Herbert Goldhamer, *Some Factors Affecting Participation in Voluntary Associations* (Ph.D. dissertation, University of Chicago, Department of Sociology, 1942).

22. Boas, *op. cit.*, p. 619.

23. *Ibid.*, p. 609.

24. Bronislaw Malinowski, *Myth in Primitive Psychology* (New York, W. W. Norton & Co., 1926).

25. Georges Sorel, *Reflections on Violence*, tr. by T. E. Hulme (New York: Peter Smith, 1941), p. 136.

26. *Ibid.*, p. 32.

27. Words of General Smuts quoted by Arnold Toynbee in *A Study of History*, abridgement of Vols. I–VI by D. C. Somervell (New York and London: Oxford University Press, 1947), p. 51.

28. *Ibid.*, p. 119.

29. These facts are given in Peter Buck's *Anthropology and Re-*

ligion (New Haven: Yale University Press; London, Oxford University Press, 1939).

30. David Kalakaua, *The Legends and Myths of Hawaii* (New York, C. L. Webster & Co., 1888).

31. Alfred Kroeber, *Anthropology* (new ed.; New York, Harcourt, Brace and Co., 1948), p. 404. In considering this Hawaiian event I have followed a lead given me by Charles Leslie, who has examined most of the sources. The principal sources are accounts written by missionaries (Dibble, Bingham, Ellis) from what was told them by natives who participated in the event.

32. Reuben Gold Thwaites, *Early Western Travels, 1748–1846* (Cleveland: Arthur H. Clark Co., 1905), XV, part ii of James' account of S. H. Long's expedition, 1819–1820, pp. 151–154. The episode is also briefly described in Rev. Jedediah Morse, *A Report to the Secretary of War of the United States on Indian Affairs,* etc. (New Haven, S. Converse, 1822), pp. 247–248.

33. According to Ralph Linton (personal communication), the Loup and the Skidi were the same.

34. Thwaites, *op. cit.,* pp. 154–155.

35. *Ibid.,* p. 153.

36. John T. Irving, *Indian Sketches, etc.* (London: John Murray, 1835), pp. 136–144.

37. Llewellyn and Hoebel, *op. cit.* The two cases mentioned here are presented and discussed on pp. 13–15; 127–129; 191.

38. Robert Redfield, *A Village that Chose Progress* (Chicago: University of Chicago Press, 1950).

39. Arthur M. Schlesinger, *The American Reformer* (Cambridge: Harvard University Press, 1950), p. 66.

40. From Emerson's essay, *Man the Reformer,* quoted in Schlesinger, *op. cit.,* p. 31.

CHAPTER VI

1. A. L. Kroeber, *Anthropology* (rev. ed.; New York: Harcourt, Brace and Co., 1948), p. 841.

2. Clyde Kluckhohn, "Values and Value-Orientations in the Theory of Action: An Exploration in Definition and Classification," *Toward a General Theory of Action,* ed. by Talcott Parsons and Edward Shils (Cambridge: Harvard University Press, 1951), pp. 388–433.

3. Raymond Firth, *Elements of Social Organization* (London: Watts and Co., 1951), pp. 183–184.

4. *Ibid.*, p. 214.

5. Kluckhohn, *op. cit.*, pp. 418–419.

6. Melville Herskovits, *Man and His Works* (New York: Alfred A. Knopf, 1948), pp. 61–78.

7. *Ibid.*, p. 63.

8. Eliseo Vivas, *The Moral Life and the Ethical Life* (Chicago: University of Chicago Press, 1950), pp. 25–42.

9. Bronislaw Malinowski, Argonauts of the Western Pacific (New York: E. P. Dutton & Co., 1950), p. 517.

10. Herskovits, *op. cit.*, p. 76.

11. *Ibid.*, p. 77.

12. H. G. Barnett, "On Science and Human Rights," *American Anthropologist*, n.s. L (April–June, 1948), 352–354.

13. David Bidney, "Question of Values: The Concept of Value in Modern Anthropology," inventory paper for Wenner-Gren Foundation International Symposium on Anthropology, New York City, June 9–20, 1952.

14. "Statement on Human Rights," *American Anthropologist*, n.s. XLIX (October–December, 1947), 539.

15. *Ibid.*, p. 542.

16. *Ibid.*, p. 543.

17. Barnett, *op. cit.*; Julian H. Steward, "Comments on the Statement on Human Rights," *American Anthropologist*, n.s. L (April–June, 1948), 351–352.

18. Steward, *op. cit.*

19. Barnett, *op. cit.*

20. And appeared to authorize anthropologists to utter statements they know to be unsound so as to reach ends they believe in as citizens. John W. Bennett, "Science and Human Rights: Reason and Action," *American Anthropologist*, n.s. LI (April–June, 1949), 329–336.

21. J. C. Furnas, *The Anatomy of Paradise* (New York: William Sloan Associates, 1937), p. 480.

22. Ruth Benedict, *Patterns of Culture* (New York: Penguin Books, 1946; first published in 1934), pp. 227–231.

23. Alfonso Villa Rojas, *Notas sobre la etnografía de los Indios Tzeltales de Oxchuc,* original field notes on a community in Chiapas, Mexico, roughly ordered by their author (microfilm collection, Department of Anthropology, University of Chicago).

24. Gordon MacGregor, *Warriors without Weapons* (Chicago: University of Chicago Press, 1946).

25. Herskovits, *op. cit.*, p. 80.

26. Firth, R. W., *Primitive Economics of the New Zealand Maori* (New York: E. P. Dutton & Co., 1929), p. xii.

27. For a view of the role of valuing in the work of the anthropologist that is consonant with that expressed in these pages, see S. F. Nadel, *The Foundations of Social Anthropology* (London: Cohen & West, 1951), pp. 48–55.

28. Furnas, *op. cit.*, p. 478.

29. Oscar Lewis, *Life in a Mexican Village: Tepoztlán Restudied* (Urbana: University of Illinois Press, 1951).

30. *Ibid.*, p. 435.

31. *Ibid.*, p. 448.

32. Furnas, *op. cit.*, p. 488.

33. Vivas, *op. cit.*, p. 35.

34. Franz Boas, "Anthropology," *Encyclopaedia of Social Sciences;* A. L. Kroeber, *op. cit.*, p. 303; and Leslie White (in the special form of increase in per capita consumption of natural power), *The Science of Culture* (New York: Farrar, Straus and Co., 1949).

35. Boas, *op. cit.*, p. 103.

36. Kroeber, *op. cit.*, p. 298.

37. *Ibid.*, p. 299.

38. *Ibid.*, p. 300.

39. *Ibid.*, p. 304.

40. *Ibid.*, p. 305.

41. *Ibid.*, p. 301.

42. *Ibid.*, p. 300.

43. *Ibid.*, p. 301.

44. Herskovits, *op. cit.*, p. 71.

◇◇◇

The Messenger Lectures

IN its original form this book consisted of six lectures delivered at Cornell University in February and March, 1952, namely, the Messenger Lectures on the Evolution of Civilization. That series was founded and its title prescribed by Hiram J. Messenger, B.Litt., Ph.D., of Hartford, Connecticut, who directed in his will that a portion of his estate be given to Cornell University and used to provide annually a "course or courses of lectures on the evolution of civilization, for the special purpose of raising the moral standard of our political, business, and social life." The lectureship was established in 1923.

❖❖❖

Index